TAPESTRY

LET'S
TALK
BUSINESS

TAPESTRY

The **Tapestry** program of language materials is based on the concepts presented in *The Tapestry of Language Learning: The Individual in the Communicative Classroom* by Robin C. Scarcella & Rebecca L. Oxford.

Each title in this program focuses on:

Individual learner strategies and instruction

The relatedness of skills

Ongoing self-assessment

Authentic material as input

Theme-based learning linked to task-based instruction

Attention to all aspects of communicative competence

TAPESTRY

LET'S TALK BUSINESS

Joni Vetrano
Elizabeth Whalley
Laurie Blass

Heinle & Heinle Publishers
An International Thomson
Publishing Company
Boston, Massachusetts, 02116, USA

I(T)P

The publication of *Let's Talk Business* was directed by the members of the Heinle & Heinle Global Innovations Publishing Team:

Elizabeth Holthaus, Global Innovations Team Leader
David C. Lee, Editorial Director
John F. McHugh, Market Development Director
Lisa McLaughlin, Production Services Coordinator

Also participating in the publication of this program were:

Director of Production: Elizabeth Holthaus
Publisher: Stanley J. Galek
Assistant Editor: Kenneth Mattsson
Manufacturing Coordinator: Mary Beth Hennebury
Full Service Project Manager/Compositor: PC&F, Inc.
Interior Design: Maureen Lauran
Cover Design: Maureen Lauran

Manufactured in the United States of America

ISBN: 0-8384-4005-3

Heinle & Heinle Publishers is an International Thomson Publishing Company.

10 9 8 7 6 5 4 3 2 1

To my talented and handsome husband, Joe;
and to my two musketeers,
Mom and Jeanne

J.V.

To the memory of Gertrude Whalley, Stanley Whalley,
Fred Goldstein, and Ann Benjamin

E.W.

To the memory of Joseph Blass

L.B.

PHOTO CREDITS

TEXT CREDITS

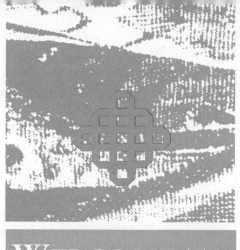

WELCOME TO TAPESTRY

*E*nter the world of Tapestry! Language learning can be seen as an ever-developing tapestry woven with many threads and colors. The elements of the tapestry are related to different language skills like listening and speaking, reading and writing; the characteristics of the teachers; the desires, needs, and backgrounds of the students; and the general second language development process. When all these elements are working together harmoniously, the result is a colorful, continuously growing tapestry of language competence of which the student and the teacher can be proud.

This volume is part of the Tapestry program for students of English as a second language (ESL) at levels from beginning to "bridge" (which follows the advanced level and prepares students to enter regular postsecondary programs along with native English speakers). Tapestry levels include:

Beginning
Low Intermediate
High Intermediate
Advanced
High Advanced
Bridge

Because the Tapestry program provides a unified theoretical and pedagogical foundation for all its components, you can optimally use all the Tapestry student books in a coordinated fashion as an entire curriculum of materials. (They will be published from 1993 to 1996 with further editions likely thereafter.) Alternatively, you can decide to use just certain Tapestry volumes, depending on your specific needs.

Tapestry is primarily designed for ESL students at postsecondary institutions in North America. Some want to learn ESL for academic or career advancement, others for social and personal reasons. Tapestry builds directly on all these motivations. Tapestry stimulates learners to do their best. It enables learners to use English naturally and to develop fluency as well as accuracy.

Tapestry Principles

The following principles underlie the instruction provided in all of the components of the Tapestry program.

EMPOWERING LEARNERS

Language learners in Tapestry classrooms are active and increasingly responsible for developing their English language skills and related cultural abilities. This self direction leads to better, more rapid learning. Some cultures virtually train their students to be passive in the classroom, but Tapestry weans them from passivity by providing exceptionally high interest materials, colorful and motivating activities, personalized self-reflection tasks, peer tutoring and other forms of cooperative learning, and powerful learning strategies to boost self direction in learning.

The empowerment of learners creates refreshing new roles for teachers, too. The teacher serves as facilitator, co-communicator, diagnostician, guide, and helper. Teachers are set free to be more creative at the same time their students become more autonomous learners.

HELPING STUDENTS IMPROVE THEIR LEARNING STRATEGIES

Learning strategies are the behaviors or steps an individual uses to enhance his or her learning. Examples are taking notes, practicing, finding a conversation partner, analyzing words, using background knowledge, and controlling anxiety. Hundreds of such strategies have been identified. Successful language learners use language learning strategies that are most effective for them given their particular learning style, and they put them together smoothly to fit the needs of a given language task. On the other hand, the learning strategies of less successful learners are a desperate grab-bag of ill-matched techniques.

All learners need to know a wide range of learning strategies. All learners need systematic practice in choosing and applying strategies that are relevant for various learning needs. Tapestry is one of the only ESL programs that overtly weaves a comprehensive set of learning strategies into language activities in all its volumes. These learning strategies are arranged in eight broad categories throughout the Tapestry books:

Forming concepts
Personalizing
Remembering new material
Managing your learning
Understanding and using emotions
Overcoming limitations
Testing Hypotheses
Learning with Others

The most useful strategies are sometimes repeated and flagged with a note, "It Works! Learning Strategy . . ." to remind students to use a learning strategy they have already encountered. This recycling reinforces the value of learning strategies and provides greater practice.

RECOGNIZING AND HANDLING LEARNING STYLES EFFECTIVELY

Learners have different learning styles (for instance, visual, auditory, hands- on; reflective, impulsive; analytic, global; extroverted, introverted; closure-oriented, open). Particularly in an ESL setting, where students come from vastly different cultural backgrounds, learning styles differences abound and can cause "style conflicts."

Unlike most language instruction materials, Tapestry provides exciting activities specifically tailored to the needs of students with a large range of learning styles. You can use any Tapestry volume with the confidence that the activities and materials are intentionally geared for many different styles. Insights from the latest educational and psychological research undergird this style-nourishing variety.

OFFERING AUTHENTIC, MEANINGFUL COMMUNICATION

Students need to encounter language that provides authentic, meaningful communication. They must be involved in real-life communication tasks that cause them to *want* and *need* to read, write, speak, and listen to English. Moreover, the tasks—to be most effective—must be arranged around themes relevant to learners.

Themes like family relationships, survival in the educational system, personal health, friendships in a new country, political changes, and protection of the environment are all valuable to ESL learners. Tapestry focuses on topics like these. In every Tapestry volume, you will see specific content drawn from very broad areas such as home life, science and technology, business, humanities, social sciences, global issues, and multiculturalism. All the themes are real and important, and they are fashioned into language tasks that students enjoy.

At the advanced level, Tapestry also includes special books each focused on a single broad theme. For instance, there are two books on business English, two on English for science and technology, and two on academic communication and study skills.

UNDERSTANDING AND VALUING DIFFERENT CULTURES

Many ESL books and programs focus completely on the "new" culture, that is, the culture which the students are entering. The implicit message is that ESL students should just learn about this target culture, and there is no need to understand their own culture better or to find out about the cultures of their international classmates. To some ESL students, this makes them feel their own culture is not valued in the new country.

Tapestry is designed to provide a clear and understandable entry into North American culture. Nevertheless, the Tapestry Program values *all* the cultures found in the ESL classroom. Tapestry students have constant opportunities to become "culturally fluent" in North American culture while they are learning English, but they also have the chance to think about the cultures of their classmates and even understand their home culture from different perspectives.

INTEGRATING THE LANGUAGE SKILLS

Communication in a language is not restricted to one skill or another. ESL students are typically expected to learn (to a greater or lesser degree) all four language skills: reading, writing, speaking, and listening. They are also expected to develop strong grammatical competence, as well as becoming socioculturally sensitive and knowing what to do when they encounter a "language barrier."

Research shows that multi-skill learning is more effective than isolated-skill learning, because related activities in several skills provide reinforcement and refresh the learner's memory. Therefore, Tapestry integrates all the skills. A given Tapestry volume might highlight one skill, such as reading, but all other skills are also included to support and strengthen overall language development.

However, many intensive ESL programs are divided into classes labeled according to one skill (Reading Comprehension Class) or at most two skills (Listening/Speaking Class or Oral Communication Class). The volumes in the Tapestry Program can easily be used to fit this traditional format, because each volume clearly identifies its highlighted or central skill(s).

Grammar is interwoven into all Tapestry volumes. However, there is also a separate reference book for students, *The Tapestry Grammar,* and a Grammar Strand composed of grammar "work-out" books at each of the levels in the Tapestry Program.

Other Features of the Tapestry Program

PILOT SITES

It is not enough to provide volumes full of appealing tasks and beautiful pictures. Users deserve to know that the materials have been pilot-tested. In many ESL series, pilot testing takes place at only a few sites or even just in the classroom of the author. In contrast, Heinle & Heinle Publishers have developed a network of Tapestry Pilot Test Sites throughout North America. At this time, there are approximately 40 such sites, although the number grows weekly. These sites try out the materials and provide suggestions for revisions. They are all actively engaged in making Tapestry the best program possible.

AN OVERALL GUIDEBOOK

To offer coherence to the entire Tapestry Program and especially to offer support for teachers who want to understand the principles and practice of Tapestry, we have written a book entitled, *The Tapestry of Language Learning. The Individual in the Communicative Classroom* (Scarcella and Oxford, published in 1992 by Heinle & Heinle).

A Last Word

We are pleased to welcome you to Tapestry! We use the Tapestry principles every day, and we hope these principles—and all the books in the Tapestry Program— provide you the same strength, confidence, and joy that they give us. We look forward to comments from both teachers and students who use any part of the Tapestry Program.

Rebecca L. Oxford
University of Alabama
Tuscaloosa, Alabama

Robin C. Scarcella
University of California at Irvine
Irvine, California

PREFACE

What Is *Let's Talk Business?*

Let's Talk Business is a dynamic business English as a Second Language text that combines basic through advanced business concepts with general and business-oriented communication skills. It can be used by students preparing to major in business, those in a business program, as well as those already in the workplace who want to improve their communication skills. *Let's Talk Business* is targeted for advanced ESL students in intensive and nonintensive programs.

Let's Talk Business fills the gap in materials available to students whose main interest is to be successful in the international business world by combining traditional business content—such as economics, marketing, management, and written and oral communication—with nontraditional content—etiquette, corporate culture, and environmental concerns. *Let's Talk Business* empowers students with the communication tools they need to succeed professionally and socially in the global marketplace.

Special Features

Let's Talk Business has these unique features:

- Hands-on business tasks and activities that simulate the real world
- Activities that allow students to practice and evaluate the subtleties of real-life communication, such as nonverbal behavior, tone, and level of formality
- Activities—both in and out of class—that are realistic, interactive, and cooperative, such as organizing and managing group events and tasks, letter and memo writing, interviews, and information gathering
- Authentic, high-interest readings from prominent business publications, such as *Forbes, Business Week, The Wall Street Journal,* and *The Economist*

- Prereading, postreading, and listening activities specifically designed to help students understand and manipulate the sophisticated concepts and complex language of authentic source materials
- Vocabulary building exercises that promote active use of idioms and key business expressions
- Learning strategies appearing throughout that help students focus on their individual learning processes and facilitate independent learning

How *Let's Talk Business* Is Organized

A typical *Let's Talk Business* chapter has the following sequence:

PART I: PREPARATION

This section introduces ideas and language through reading passages and activities that give students a broad view of the chapter's basic business concepts and related language. It winds up by establishing goals, and allowing students to express their personal goals for the chapter. In this way students become invested in the learning process and in the topic and discover how to take control of their own learning.

PART II: INTEGRATION

Part II includes in-depth coverage of two or three aspects of the chapter topic through reading or listening passages with real-life examples that illustrate business concepts. These passages are supported by follow-up activities that

- develop reading and listening comprehension and promote critical thinking skills.
- help students personalize concepts.
- highlight relevant, practical business terminology, including buzzwords and jargon.
- allow students to integrate and synthesize material from the entire chapter and put it to use in new, real-life situations.

PART III: EVALUATION

The Evaluation section helps students review and suggests ways to expand chapter and personal goals. It gives them the opportunity to demonstrate how well they've met their objectives and to consider further investigation of the chapter topic.

Acknowledgments

We would like to express our gratitude to the prime movers of the *Tapestry* series: Dave Lee, Rebecca Oxford, and Robin Scarcella. We are also indebted to Ken Mattsson for his support of and dedication to us and to the project. In addition, we gratefully acknowledge the significant contributions of Betty Floreani during the early stages of this project.

We would also like to thank Sam Petrovich, Lanny Lampl, David Blass, Paul Durighello, Ann Pongracz, Craig Lee, Sandra Stumbaugh, and Larry Alexander; the folks down at the plant: Dorothy Bender; Claude Baudoin; Peter Detkin; Ed Felts, Linda, Melina, and Oscar Platus; Frank Koenig and Gray Clossman; Alice, Barr, Megan, and Suesan Taylor; and the group who rarely go to the plant: Mary Dunn; Sue Marritt Garfield; Chris, Osha, Michael, Robert, and Seraph Hanling, Manouso Manos; Lewis Leavitt; and Debra Satz.

Finally, we would like to acknowledge the contributions of the reviewers who provided valuable input during the development of this project: Marcia Cassidy, Miami-Dade Community College; Patrick Chalmers, Governors State University; Steve Horowitz, Central Washingon University; Mary Ann Julian, University of California at Berkeley; Robert Irwin, Center for English Studies (NY); Patrick Oglesby, Duke University; Melissa Tawalbeh, University of Findlay; and the San Francisco, Palo Alto, and Contra Costa Public Library systems for the help provided by their personnel and materials.

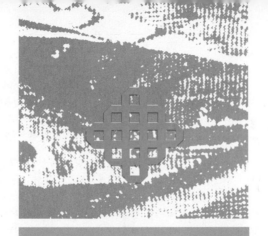

CONTENTS

6 Marketing: Products and Services for Today's Consumer   87

7 Investing in High Tech   109

8 Environmental Issues in Business   127

9

Startup Businesses: The Entrepreneurial Spirit 147

10

Global Economics and You 167

Business Etiquette

In this chapter, you'll

- practice appropriate behavior when meeting someone for the first time in a business setting.
- understand and practice using tone in order to be polite.
- understand and practice formality levels in English.
- understand and practice nonverbal communication.

Threads

Manners: 50% common sense, 50% thinking about someone else.

People are more at ease with machines than each other.
—Letitia Baldrige

In North America, as in all countries, business situations have unspoken "rules" of behavior. In this chapter, you will learn some of these rules: how to use the quality of your voice to make a good impression, what vocabulary is appropriate in a business setting, and how body language is part of good conversation. In addition, you will learn about U.S. business protocol—that is, fixed rules of behavior for particular situations.

PART I

Preparation

LEARNING STRATEGY

Forming Concepts: Predicting what you will hear makes a listening passage easier to understand.

A. BRAINSTORMING

Answer the following questions on your own. Then discuss your answers with a business team.

1. How do you define "manners"?
2. What is your opinion of American manners?

B. WORKING WITH CONCEPTS: THE STATE OF AMERICAN MANNERS

Listen to a talk Letitia Baldrige gave to a group of business people on "Manners in the '90s." Ms. Baldrige is an expert on manners, and in the 1960s was chief of staff to Jacqueline Kennedy in the White House.

[Now, listen to the speaker.]

C. JARGON, BUZZWORDS, AND SLANG: BUSINESS ETIQUETTE

Match the expressions from Baldrige's talk on the left with their definitions on the right.

Expressions

not so hot
self-assuredness
being "cool"

common sense

mercenary
being a klutz

Definitions

being clumsy
doing something only for the money
good judgment that does not depend on book learning
behaving in an acceptable way within a social group
not so good
self confidence

LEARNING STRATEGY

Remembering New Material: Associating new words with words you already know helps you remember vocabulary.

Now write your own definitions for these terms:

1. not so hot
2. self-assuredness
3. being "cool"
4. common sense
5. mercenary
6. being a klutz

D. PUTTING IT ALL TOGETHER

1. Following are some situations that call for proper etiquette—common sense or consideration of others. On a sheet of paper, write what *you* would do in these situations. Then ask a native English speaker what he or she recommends and write that answer below yours.

   a. You are talking to people in a group. Someone you know comes up to the group. What should you do?

   b. You are about to introduce your manager, and you forget his or her name. What should you do?

   c. You arrive late for a meeting that you don't consider very important. What should you do?

   d. You arrive late for a meeting that is very important. What should you do?

   e. You are working hard on a project for your boss, and a senior executive walks into your office. What should you do?

2. Choose one of the preceding situations and role-play it with your business team. Perform the role-play for another business team at a company meeting.

E. DEBRIEFING MEETING

Discuss your results for Exercise D at a company meeting. Consider the following questions:

- To what extent did your answers differ from a native English speaker's?
- Which answer surprised you the most? Why?
- Which answer surprised you the least? Why?

Also, discuss how associates from different countries handled each situation.

F. SETTING OBJECTIVES

Following are the goals for this chapter. Read them, and consider your personal goals. At the end of this chapter, on page 14, you'll list your results.

OBJECTIVES

Business
1. To distinguish social from business settings
2. To practice the appropriate behavior on meeting someone for the first time

Language
3. To understand and practice using a good voice and a cultivated vocabulary
4. To understand and practice formality levels of language
5. To understand and practice tone
6. To understand and practice nonverbal communication
7. To practice giving advice using *should, ought to*, and *had better*

Personal

_____

_____

_____

Integration

A. THE ART OF SUCCESSFUL COMMUNICATION

How you talk and what you say are a big part of good manners. In Letitia Baldrige's *Complete Guide to Executive Manners,* she discusses the importance of how you sound to the outside world. Before you read an excerpt from Baldrige, answer the following questions:

LEARNING STRATEGY

Remembering New Material: Figuring out what you already know about a topic before you read about it saves you time.

1. What kind of voice makes a person sound secure?
2. What kind of voice lends authority to what a person is saying?
3. What is the problem with speaking too quickly?
4. What is the problem with speaking too slowly?
5. Should you use common slang in a business setting? Why or why not?
6. How close should you stand to someone when you meet them?
7. How can you communicate that you are listening to a speaker when you are sitting down?

Now read the following passage:

COMPLETE GUIDE TO EXECUTIVE MANNERS
by Letitia Baldrige

A pleasant-sounding voice is a great asset in business and social life: People want to listen to what you have to say.

YOUR VOICE IS GOOD IF:	YOUR VOICE NEEDS IMPROVING IF:
It is clear and your diction is clear.	It is difficult to understand and your words are not properly enunciated.
You have a low, comfortable pitch—that of a secure person.	Your pitch is too high, makimg you sound immature or nervous.
You have a clear tone, which lends authority to what you are saying.	Your tone is harsh and sounds strident and unreasonable.
You sound well-paced, not too fast nor too slow. (Voice monotony should be avoided at all costs.)	You displease the listener, either because you go too fast to be understood, or too slow to be interesting.
You have a warm, intimate, vital quality	You sound cold and uncaring.
It expresses emotion—such as sympathy and enthusiasm.	Your tone is flat and seemingly unmoved by anything.

Threads

Letitia Baldrige recommends that you learn these phrases for any country you are planning to visit: Hello. Good-bye. Please. Delighted to meet you. I'm sorry. I'm having a great time. I hope you are well. Please come and visit us. Thank you so much. No, thank you. My company makes (or does) such-and-such. We are a big (or small) company. That is very impressive.

A Cultivated Voice Implies a Cultivated Vocabulary

In reality a cultivated voice is:

- Noted for the absence of foul language
- One that does not tediously feature repetitious phrases (for example: "Know what I mean?" "Isn't that so?" or just "You know?")
- One in which common slang is absent. For example, starting every sentence with "Like" is totally ungrammatical. So is "I'm into aerobics" or "I'm into cooking." Things should be called by their proper names. Liquor is liquor, not "booze." Money is money, not "bucks" or "moola."

Good Body Language Is Part of Good Conversation

Body language is a personal thing. It tells a lot about a person's character, such as whether he shows respect for others to whom he is talking, and whether he pays proper attention to someone's else's ideas.

Think about your own body language. Be conscious of it. For example: When you meet someone, don't stand too close. (Remember the angry expression, "Stay out of my face!") An uncomfortable closeness is very annoying to the other person, so keep your physical distance, or he'll have to keep backing off from you. A minimum of two feet will do it.

Some of the ways in which your body will tell the other person you are listening intently are these:

You sit attentively in your chair. If you slump down on your backbone, your legs straight out in front of you, your body is saying, "I don't care what you're saying, and frankly, you bore me."

You watch the face of the person speaking and do not let your eyes roam randomly around the room. It's polite to give the person speaking your full attention in a "do unto others as you would have others do unto you" kind of philosophy.

You keep your legs still, not continuously shifting your position or crossing and uncrossing your knees. The latter body language signifies either aching joints or the fact that you can hardly wait to get away. Letting your knee bounce up and down continuously also denotes boredom with the present company, which is the way you may feel, but you should certainly disguise that fact.

Source: Adapted from *Letitia Baldrige's New Complete Guide to Executive Manners.* Rawson Associates, New York. 1993. Pp. 114–116; 121–122.

B. ANALYZING WHAT YOU'VE READ

With your business team, answer the following questions about the passage you just read.

1. What are the characteristics of a good voice for an executive?
2. In the formal language of a business setting, several things are missing that are often found in "street language," or everyday speech. What are they?
3. Where do you look when someone is talking?
4. What do you communicate if you keep crossing and uncrossing your legs when someone is speaking?

C. TONE, FORM, AND BODY LANGUAGE

LEARNING STRATEGY

Remembering New Material: Classifying words helps you remember them.

1. Some of the terms Baldrige uses have positive meanings, while others are negative or neutral. Use a checkmark (√) to classify the italicized words in the following phrases as Positive (+) or Negative (−).

WORD	+	−
clear diction	√	
sound *immature*		
harsh tone		
strident tone		
voice *monotony*		
well-paced		
tone is *flat*		
foul language		
common *slang*		
low pitch		

LEARNING STRATEGY

Managing Your Learning: Acting out the meaning of words helps you understand them.

2. With a business team, act out the following terms as you say "Thursday will be an unusual and interesting day": strident tone, voice monotony, and clear diction. Then, paraphrase the sentence using slang.

LEARNING STRATEGY

Personalizing: Thinking of examples on your own or with an associate helps you better understand new material.

3. In business, people rarely use foul language such as "What the hell," "I don't give a damn," or "That's a lot of crap." Make a list of expressions that would *not* be acceptable in a formal business setting. (If writing these words makes you uncomfortable, just indicate the first letters of the words you are thinking of, e.g., s—, f—, etc.)

4. In business settings, people also avoid common slang. Slang is always changing. Ask three English speakers about your own age to give you six to ten slang expressions they use. Ask them what they would say when they want to say something is "really good," "really bad," or when they want to show they are angry or frustrated. Then ask them if those expressions would be appropriate in a business setting. Make a chart, using the following format:

PERSON #1   APPROXIMATE AGE: _____

Expressions:	Appropriate in a business setting:
_____	_____
_____	_____
_____	

D. DEBRIEFING MEETING

In a company meeting, discuss the foul language and slang that you obtained in Exercise C. For every expression that is not appropriate in a business setting, suggest a substitute expression.

Communication Memo • Communication Memo • Communication Memo

To: All Employees
From: Corporate Communications Department
Re: Use of modals: *should, ought to, had better*

In a business setting, managers often ask each other for advice. In order to give advice effectively and observe rules of correct business etiquette, please review the following information:

- *Should* and *ought to* are used to give advice. For example:

  You *should* use a round table at the meeting, so we can all see the speaker. You *ought to* use a round table at the meeting, so we can all see the speaker.

- *Had bette*r is stronger than *should* or *ought to*. Use *had better* when you want to sound forceful. It's almost impolite to use *had better* with a superior. For example:

  You *had better* use a round table at the meeting, so we can all see the speaker.

- You can, however, use *had better* as a contraction with an expression such as *perhaps, I think,* or *maybe* to make your suggestion sound more like a suggestion than a command. For example:

  Perhaps you'd better use a round table at the meeting, so we can all see each speaker.
  I think you'd better use a round table at the meeting, so we can all see each speaker.
  Maybe you'd better use a round table at the meeting, so we can all see each speaker.

Please fill out the enclosed attachment and return it to your department head.

GG/ew
Enc.

Memo Attachment

With an associate, read the following requests for advice and make suggestions using *should, ought to,* or *had better*.

1. Frank, an associate: "What do you think I should do? I have theater tickets on the night of our office Christmas Party."
2. June, an associate: "What do you think I should do? Tim asked me to pick him up at the airport at 10 P.M. and I'm usually in bed by 9:30."
3. Robert, your manager: "I'm going to your country next week. Should I bring some presents with me for the managers I'll meet there?"
4. Steve Swanson, Robert's manager: "I'm going to your country next week, and I'm invited for dinner. Should I arrive early, just on time, or late?"
5. Thomas Stern, the president of the company: "I'm going to your country next week, and I wonder if I should talk about politics or if I should avoid that topic."

E. PUTTING IT ALL TOGETHER

In your business team, role-play the following: You are planning a meeting to make plans for the company bonus party. At this party a "bonus"—additional money—will be given to each member of the company. At the meeting you should decide whether:

- the bonus party will be formal or informal;
- the party will be outdoors or indoors;
- it will be in the morning, afternoon, or evening;
- every member of the company should get the same bonus, or the bonus should depend on the employee's current salary, or it should be tied to how long someone has been with the company.

The possible participants in the role play are: Frank, an associate; June, an associate; Robert, a manager; Steve Swanson, Robert's manager; and Thomas Stern, the president of the company.

Choose one or two associates to take notes on the level of formality of the language, the tone, and the body language of the participants in the role-play. Use the following chart:

FEATURE	APPROPRIATE	INAPPROPRIATE	COMMENTS AND SUGGESTIONS
Form			
Tone			
Nonverbal behavior			

F. "DON'T MIX BUSINESS WITH PLEASURE"

In business, it's sometimes difficult to tell where the business world ends and the social world begins.

Read the following excerpt, "How to Tell Business from Social Life," from *Miss Manners' Guide for the Turn-of-the Millennium,* by Judith Martin, the internationally syndicated author of the "Miss Manners" column. Look for areas in which you agree and disagree with Miss Manners.

HOW TO TELL BUSINESS FROM SOCIAL LIFE
by Judith Martin

Many people cannot distinguish their business lives from their social lives anymore. The people are the same; the conversation is the same; the only difference is how the groceries are billed. You know it's a business occasion if you can put it on the expense account; if you have to go to the trouble of paying for it and then trying to justify deducting it from your taxes as a necessary professional expenditure, it's considered your social life.

This is awful. Miss Manners sees great progress in the fact that ladies and gentlemen can pursue many different occupations, not just the traditional ones of exploiting serfs and marrying money, but it dismays her that they have forgotten how to act like ladies and gentlemen.

Here are some reminders:

You do not use your own house or that of a friend to make business contacts, collect free advice, or publicize your achievements. Social occasions are for making romantic contacts, offering free advice to people not present, such as the President on what to do about the economy, and publicizing your children's achievements. You do not take out business cards at social events. There is such a thing as a social card, which may be used, but it carries only your name, and not your Telex, logo, slogan, and the address of your London office. You do not quiz other people, beyond the few pleasantries that help you pick a topic of conversation, on the subject of their occupations or employers, even if you are willing to put in "How fascinating!" at regular intervals. Well-bred people go about socially for recreation, not to seek opportunities to complain or brag about their jobs.

Source: Excerpted from *Miss Manners' Guide for the Turn of the Millennium*, Judith Martin. Pharos Books, New York. 1989. P. 383.

G. ANALYZING WHAT YOU'VE READ

Give examples of areas in which you agree and disagree with Miss Manners.

AGREE	DISAGREE
_____	_____
_____	_____
_____	_____
_____	_____
_____	_____
_____	_____
_____	_____

Compare your responses with those of an associate.

H. BUSINESS ETIQUETTE

Write Miss Manners' terms from her article in the blank after its definition.

Terms
expense account
professional expenditure
marrying money
pleasantries
well-bred
brag

Definitions

a. exaggerate your own good qualities: _brag_____

b. small talk: _____

c. well brought up: _____

d. marrying someone who is rich: _____

e. business expense: _____

f. an account for business expenses: _____

LEARNING STRATEGY

Personalizing: Thinking of examples from your own life helps you understand concepts.

I. PUTTING IT ALL TOGETHER

1. Give three examples of occasions that are clearly business occasions, and explain why.
2. Give three examples of occasions that are clearly social occasions, and explain why.
3. Give three examples of occasions that are a mix of business and socializing, and explain why.

J. LISTENING: U.S. PROTOCOL— BUSINESS AND PERSONAL

You are going to listen to advice for Americans traveling around the world from the book *Do's and Taboos Around the World.* The book also gives tips to incoming visitors. Listen one time for advice on the following:

- timing
- shaking hands
- gestures

[Now, listen to the speaker.]

Now listen again and answer these questions:

1. If an appointment is called for 9 A.M. sharp in Minneapolis, at what time do things actually begin?
2. If an appointment is called for 9 A.M. sharp in Los Angeles, at what time do things actually begin?
3. If an invitation says "drinks at seven," at what time can you arrive and not be considered late?
4. If an invitation says "dinner at eight," what time does dinner actually begin?
5. When you meet a woman in a business setting, should you shake her hand?
6. With an associate, demonstrate the following:
   a. That he or she has a phone call
   b. That you wish your associate "good luck"
   c. That you are leaving

K. PUTTING IT ALL TOGETHER

1. Plan and carry out a business event. In business teams of three or four, organize one of the following:
   • A business lunch at a restaurant
   • A business dinner at a restaurant or at someone's home
   • A breakfast meeting

   Take roles (e.g., president, head of sales, director of research, director of human resources, engineering team manager) and plan an agenda in which you have four or five items to accomplish (e.g., a company policy on job sharing, how to save money either by firing two people or cutting everyone's hours). Report the results of your event at a company meeting.

2. Interview someone who has worked in business (e.g., a friend, a family member, a fellow student, a member of a host family). Ask him or her to talk about business etiquette at a company where that person has worked. Take notes on your interview, and share your results with your business team. You can use the following questionnaire for the interview, or think of your own questions:

   NOTE Put your questions in the past tense if the interviewee is no longer working at the company he or she is describing.

Name (optional): _____

Company Name (optional): _____

1. Describe a co-worker who is very polite. In what way is he or she polite?
2. Describe a time when a co-worker was impolite. What happened?
3. What people in the company do you call by their first name? Last name?
4. Has a co-worker ever been *un*intentionally rude? If yes, why do you think it happened?
5. What advice about etiquette would you give to someone from another country?

Evaluation

How well did you achieve the objectives for this chapter? List your results on a sheet of paper. Use the prompts that accompany each objective.

OBJECTIVES	RESULTS
Business 1. To distinguish social from business settings 2. To practice the appropriate behavior on meeting someone for the first time **Language** 3. To understand and practice using a good voice and a cultivated vocabulary 4. To understand and practice formality levels of language 5. To understand and practice tone 6. To understand and practice nonverbal communication 7. To practice giving advice using *should, ought to,* and *had better* **Personal** _____ _____ _____	**Business** 1. Give an example of a situation that is strictly a business situation, and one that is strictly social. 2. Describe what you do when you meet someone for the first time. **Language** 3. List two qualities of a good voice. Give one example of cultivated vocabulary. 4. Give a common slang expression and its formal equivalent. 5. Say the following sentence with a tone that expresses authority: "Please have a seat over there." 6. Explain how nonverbal communication can show a speaker you are paying attention. 7. Write three sentences giving advice using *should, ought to,* and *had better.* **Personal** _____ _____ _____

Now answer the following questions:

• What are your strengths in the area of etiquette?
• How can you continue to learn about etiquette on your own?

Oral Communication

CHAPTER PREVIEW

In this chapter, you'll

- learn how to introduce a business associate in a social situation.
- understand the importance of and practice making small talk with an associate, customer, or client.
- learn how to prepare an oral presentation.
- discover what conversation topics are appropriate and inappropriate with a disabled person.

Threads

Words are what hold society together.

Stuart Chase, *Consumers' Research*

It usually takes me more than three weeks to prepare a good impromptu speech.

—Mark Twain, 1835–1910, American author and riverboat captain

Oral communication—talking—is one of the main ways business "gets done" all over the world. In this chapter, you will learn some of the finer points of oral communication: how to introduce a business associate in a social situation, how to make small talk, and how to prepare an oral presentation.

PART I

Preparation

A. BRAINSTORMING

With your business team, think of the ways people communicate orally in the workplace (e.g., greeting one another first thing in the morning or inviting a co-worker to lunch). On a sheet of paper, list as many kinds of oral communication as you can think of, and mention the time and frequency of occurrence (e.g., greeting one another first thing in the morning every day, or inviting a co-worker to lunch once, twice, or more times a week).

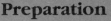

LEARNING STRATEGY

Managing Your Learning: Making your own list of information you know about a topic helps you prepare for a reading.

Compare your list with those of the other business teams. Then make a master list that includes all the ideas of business communication mentioned.

Now consider your own abilities in oral communication:

1. In which areas are you strongest?
2. In which arcas do you feel you need the most improvement?

Next, listen to Letitia Baldrige's comments on communication protocol (fixed rules of behavior for particular situations) and problems in a speech she delivered at the Commonwealth Club of California:

[Now, listen to the speaker.]

B. ANALYZING WHAT YOU'VE HEARD

LEARNING STRATEGY

Remembering New Material: Reviewing what you have learned helps you remember the information later when you need it for an exam or a real-life situation.

1. When you meet someone, nonverbal communication is very important. What aspect of nonverbal communication does Baldrige mention?
2. When you introduce someone, Baldrige suggests that you give three pieces of information about the person. What are they?
3. Baldrige has a suggestion for shy people on how to make conversation. What does she suggest that they do?
4. Baldrige says that there are certain sections of the newspaper that young people prefer to read. What are they?

C. JARGON, BUZZWORDS, AND SLANG: SMALL TALK

Write the correct terms from Baldrige's talk in the following spaces. Check your answers with an associate.

Terms
gadget
TV listings
protocol
flattering
out-of-towner
buddy

1. Susie is my friend. She really is a good _____ *buddy* _____.
2. We are in Toronto. Stephen lives in Seattle. He is a(n) _____.
3. "Good Morning America" is on every morning starting at 7 A.M. I know because I looked in the _____.
4. A TV remote control is a(n) _____.
5. "That tie is really good-looking" is a comment that's intended to be _____.
6. Seat the guest of honor on your right, the next most important person on your left, is one of the rules of _____.

D. PUTTING IT ALL TOGETHER

Understanding and Using Emotions: Rehearsing a future situation will give you confidence when you actually face a similar situation.

1. Make an identity for yourself. Give yourself a name. (You can use your own name if you wish.) Also give yourself a job title, and a sport or hobby. Write down the information on a piece of paper and hand it to an associate on your business team. Now, using the information you have been given, introduce each other to the other members of the business team.

2. In the following box, list some of the rules of protocol in your country for:
   a. An informal party (e.g., a birthday party)
   b. A more formal party (e.g., a holiday party at the office)

	INFORMAL	FORMAL
Kind of party:	_____	_____
Place:	_____	_____
Number of people invited:	_____	_____
Length of party (in hours):	_____	_____
What should people wear?:	_____	_____
How do you greet your host/hostess?	_____	_____
Can someone bring a guest? Why or why not?	_____	_____
Kind of food:	_____	_____
Music? If so, what kind?	_____	_____
Dancing?	_____	_____
What do you say when you leave, and who do you say it to?	_____	_____

E. DEBRIEFING MEETING

Compare your answers with an associate:

1. If your associate is from your country, what points do you agree on? Which do you disagree on?
2. If your associate is from another country, what points do you agree on? Which do you disagree on?

F. SETTING OBJECTIVES

Following are the goals for this chapter. Read them, and consider your personal goals. At the end of this chapter, on page 29, you'll list your results.

OBJECTIVES

Business
1. To understand the importance of and practice making conversation (including small talk) with an associate, customer, or client in business and social situations
2. To learn how to prepare an oral presentation for a business situation
3. To learn how to introduce a business associate in a social situation
4. To discover what conversation topics are appropriate and inappropriate with a disabled person in business settings

Language
5. To understand and practice using tag questions

Personal

_____

_____

_____

PART II

Integration

A. SPOKEN COMMUNICATION: WAYS OF SPEAKING AND LISTENING

Norma Carr-Ruffino has sold more than 100,000 copies of her book, *The Promotable Woman,* which is designed to help women who are not familiar with the "man's world" of business. In fact, this book is useful to *anyone* not familiar with the U.S./Canadian business scene. You are going to read an excerpt called "Sharpening Your Basic Skills" from her chapter, "Communicating Effectively." Before you read, discuss the following question with an associate and write your answer on a sheet of paper:

• What are some specific techniques you are aware of for communicating clearly with people at work?

SHARPENING YOUR BASIC SKILLS
by Norma Carr-Ruffino

The spoken word can be a powerful tool for gaining and using personal power. Therefore, it will pay to continually sharpen your skills in persuading people and in getting through to them with clear instructions, questions, and responses. Keep developing skills in tuning in to the other person's viewpoint and gearing your messages accordingly. And remain aware of your responsibility as boss for taking the initiative to establish lines of communication with your people and to keep lines open. Let's review some suggestions for sharpening these basic communication skills.

Practice Empathy. To be aware of what your listener will value as a payoff, try to put yourself in his or her shoes. How is your listener likely to feel about your message? What pressures is he or she under? How calm and confident is he or she feeling? What kind of relationship do you have? If the topic is controversial, is there anything the two of you <u>can</u> agree on to begin with?

Develop the Art of Persuasion. Remember that people usually base actions more on feeling, opinions, and beliefs than on logic and reason. A rational approach is one that considers all the variables, and in most situations there are many variables we cannot be sure of. True rationality also considers people's emotions and other "illogical" factors. Here is a five-step sequence for persuasive communication:

1. Establish rapport. Communicate to the listener, in both words and actions, that you see the problem or situation from his or her viewpoint, too.
2. Introduce your proposal or idea and suggest how it can help generally.
3. Try to determine what your listener's problems are and what payoffs are important to him or her by using good questioning techniques.
4. Follow up with details to convince. Provide the listener with evidence that your proposal can help.
5. Maintain your credibility by avoiding too many strong adjectives, adverbs, superlatives, euphemisms, or worn-out phrases; words that imply a certain knowledge of future events; and inappropriate surprise or amazement.

Watch Word Choice. Be yourself and use language you are comfortable with, but modify it to fit the situation and your listener. Choose familiar nontechnical words when talking with people who might not understand technical terms or business jargon. Make this your goal: words and statements that are as short, simple, direct, familiar, and concise as is appropriate for the listener and the situation.

Use Specific Language. Another barrier to complete communication is the use of vague, abstract, general language. The more specific your message is, the more likely the listener is to interpret it correctly. You have a picture in your mind of what you're trying to get across. The more specific the language you use to describe that picture, the more likely the listener will be to get the same picture in his or her mind. Let's look at some comparisons:

<u>General</u>: We have to get on the ball.
<u>Specific</u>: Everyone in the Field Audit unit must increase his order production by at least 5 percent.

<u>General</u>: You can bring me the stuff now.
<u>Specific</u>: I'm ready to go over the Western Region account files now.

<u>General</u>: Some people are taking advantage of my good nature.
<u>Specific</u>: Both Jim and Bob have been leaving 20 or 30 minutes early several times a week for the past month.

<u>General</u>: It's time I got what I deserve for all the hard work I do.
<u>Specific</u>: Since I achieved all the objectives we have agreed on—and even exceeded two of them—I think I deserve a $4,000-a-year raise.

Notice that in order to be specific, it's important to use the names of things ("the Western Region account files"), names of people, and numbers where possible. Watch how you use indefinite words such as "there," "that," "this," "it," "thing," "whatchamacallit," "dilly." Even when you use "he," "she," or "they," be sure you are clear about exactly whom you're referring to.

Allow for Face-Saving. The listener may or may not be aware of gaps in a message. Someone who is aware may be unwilling to ask for more information for fear of appearing ignorant or stupid. As the speaker, then, it is often crucial that you make sure your message is clear and complete. For example, you can say, "Let's review. Will you give me your interpretation of what I just said so that I can be sure I have covered everything?"

On the other hand, when you are the listener, don't resort to face-saving tactics when you are unclear about a message. Feeling free to say you don't understand can be a sign of confidence. Certainly no one signals a lack of confidence more clearly than the person who is pretending to understand.

Excerpted from *The Promotable Woman,* by Norma Carr-Ruffino.
Wadsworth Publishing Company, 1993. Pp. 218–219; 220.

B. ANALYZING WHAT YOU'VE READ

Write your answers to the following questions on a sheet of paper and compare them with an associate's answers:

1. Carr-Ruffino suggests that it is important to be good at oral communication. Why does she feel it is important to keep working to improve oral communication skills?
2. In this reading, Carr-Ruffino lists five major pieces of advice. What are they?
3. When suggesting that you "practice empathy," Carr-Ruffino suggests that it is important to consider the kind of relationship you have with the person you are talking with. Do you agree? Why or why not?
4. Why do you think Carr-Ruffino recommends that you avoid strong adjectives, superlatives, and inappropriate surprise or amazement?
5. If you are a listener and you do not understand what is being said, what does Carr-Ruffino recommend that you do? Why do you think she makes that suggestion? Do you agree with her? Why or why not?

C. JARGON, BUZZWORDS, AND SLANG: WAYS OF SPEAKING AND LISTENING

1. Choose the correct term from Carr-Ruffino's excerpt and write it in the spaces next to the paraphrases—words that mean the same thing.

   Terms

put yourself in someone else's shoes	controversial	stuff
	rapport	watchamacallit
initiative	euphemism	good nature
payoff	get on the ball	

   a. thingamajig: _watchamacallit_

   b. substitution of an indirect expression for a direct one, e.g., "kicked the bucket" or "passed away" for died: _____

   c. the action of beginning something: _____

   d. positive result of some action: _____

   e. to be in harmony, sympathy, or agreement with someone: _____

   f. any unspecified substance: _____

   g. get organized: _____

   h. put yourself in someone else's place: _____

   i. subject to debate, something that inspires differing opinions: _____

   j. generosity and kindness: _____

2. On a separate sheet, write your responses to the following, and then share them with an associate:

   a. When have you put yourself in someone else's shoes? Give an example.

   b. Give an example of one time when you or someone you know showed initiative.

   c. What will be the payoff for you if you learn English really well?

   d. What topics are controversial in your country? Which ones are also controversial in the U.S. and Canada?

   e. With what kind of person do you find you have a good rapport?

   f. What are euphemisms for the following items? (You can use either English or a translation from your own language. If you use your own language, be certain to note what your native language is.)

   - get married
   - fail
   - get drunk
   - food

   g. If you were to tell someone to "get on the ball," what kind of a relationship would you have with that person?

   h. What "stuff" would make good souvenirs to take from North America back to your country? Or what "stuff" would you suggest people bring from your country to North America? (Or what "stuff" do you usually take with you when you go to the beach?)

   i. Ray said, "Do you have a watchamacallit?—you know, that thing you use to hit a nail?" What does Ray want?

   j. Give an example of your good nature. Or give an example of the good nature of someone you know.

IT WORKS!
Learning Strategy:
Thinking of
Examples from
Your Own Life

Communication Memo • Communication Memo • Communication Memo

To: All Employees
From: Corporate Communications Department
Re: Understanding and using tag questions to establish rapport

As you know, when you are communicating orally, it is useful to establish rapport with your listener. Using tag questions is one way to do this. Please review the following three kinds of tag questions in order to use them correctly and understand them when other people use them.

- You can use tags in real questions. For example:
  Sam: "The meeting doesn't begin at eight, does it?"
  (Note the rising intonation on the tag question.)

  In this example, Sam really wants to know when the meeting begins. (And he's probably hoping that it isn't early in the morning.)

- You can use tags in informative questions—questions that give or confirm information. For example:
  Sam: The meeting begins at eight, doesn't it?
  (Note the falling intonation on the tag question.)

  In this example, Sam knows that the meeting begins at eight and wants to make certain the listener is informed also.

- You can use tags in hostile questions. For example:
  Sam: He thinks he deserves a raise, does he?
  (Note the sharply rising intonation on the tag question.)

  In this example, Sam is angry that an employee wants a raise.

Using the following attachment as a guide, practice the three kinds of questions.

CM/pb
Enc.

Memo Attachment

First, practice the three kinds of intonation in the Communication Memo in a company meeting. Then, with an associate, practice saying the following sentences with the kind of intonation suggested.

Example: Information intonation:
Quality control is in the main building, isn't it?

1. Informative intonation: Shipping is on the fourth floor, isn't it?
2. Real question intonation: Shipping is on the fourth floor, isn't it?
3. Hostile intonation: He's late again, is he?
4. Real question intonation: Your product will be available on the 14th, won't it?
5. Informative intonation: We have performance evaluations on Friday, don't we?
6. Hostile intonation: He says he's leaving early, does he?

D. PUTTING IT ALL TOGETHER

1. You are going to practice persuasion. Imagine you and your associates work for a medium-sized company. Choose to argue for one of the following controversial issues that will affect your company:
   • Remodeling the old building versus building a new one
   • Keeping the company where you are now, or moving it abroad where labor costs are cheaper
   • Becoming an employee-owned company
   • Other (your choice)

   Half of the business teams take one side, and half take the other side of the controversy. Make a list of arguments for your side. Then work with your team to prepare to argue for your side. To prepare, write down on a sheet of paper how you will do the following:

   a. Establish rapport
   b. Suggest how your point of view will be generally helpful
   c. Figure out what problems the other side will have with your point of view
   d. List the arguments you will use to convince the other side

   Now, practice presenting your side's point of view to the members of your business team. Then choose someone on your team to present your side's point of view to another business team.
   Use the following chart to rate the speaker from the other business team when he or she comes to your group.

FEATURE	APPROPRIATE	INAPPROPRIATE	COMMENTS AND SUGGESTIONS
Form			
Tone			
Nonverbal behavior			

E. ORAL COMMUNICATION: STRUCTURING A PRESENTATION

Just as there is a structure to a baseball game, a theater presentation or a concert, there is a structure to an oral presentation. Learning this structure will make preparing and giving oral presentations easier. You are going to read a selection called "Structuring a Presentation," from Mary Munter's *Guide to Managerial Communication,* which describes how to structure an oral presentation and how oral presentations are different from written communication.
Before you read, discuss your answer to this question with an associate: How do you think oral presentations differ from written communication?

STRUCTURING A PRESENTATON

by Mary Munter

Presenting information orally differs from presenting it in writing. An effective presentation structure includes (1) an opening, (2) a preview of the main points, (3) clearly demarcated main points, and (4) a closing.

Use an effective opening. Openings are important in all forms of communication. When you make an oral presentation, however, your opening is even more crucial than it is when you write. Unlike your readers, who decide when and where to read your document, your listeners have had the time and place imposed on them; they are likely to have other things on their minds. Therefore, speech communication experts advise using your first minute or two of a presentation for your opening.

<u>Goals.</u> Your opening should accomplish any of the following four goals that have not already been met: (1) It should arouse your audience's interest, especially if their initial interest is low; (2) it should show how the topic relates to them, especially if that relationship isn't immediately apparent; (3) if you are unknown to the audience or have low credibility, it should establish why you're competent to talk about the subject; and (4) it should give you a chance to establish rapport with your audience.

<u>Alternative</u> <u>techniques.</u> To meet these goals, consider using one or more of these techniques to compose your opening. (1) <u>Use humor</u>. When most people think of an opening, they think of telling a joke. Actually you don't necessarily have to be humorous or entertaining in your opening. Use humor only if it fits your personality and style, if it is appropriate for every member of the audience, and if it relates to the specific topic or occasion. (2) <u>Refer to the unusual.</u> You might open by referring to something unusual. Examples would include a rhetorical question, a promise of what your presentation will deliver, a vivid image, a startling example or story, or an important statistic. (3) <u>Refer to the familiar</u>. You might open your presentation by referring to something familiar to your audience, something they can easily relate to. Examples of this kind of opening include a reference to your audience (who they are), to the occasion (why you are there), to the relationship between the audience and the subject, or to someone or something familiar to the audience.

Next, give a preview. A preview is a table of contents, an agenda, an outline of what you will be covering in your presentation. Think about the contrast between listeners and readers. Your readers can skim a document, see how long it is, and read your headings and subheadings before they start reading. Your listeners, by contrast, have no idea what you will be covering unless you tell them. One of the most common problems in business presentation is the lack of a preview. Always give an explicit preview before you begin discussing your main points.

In the most formal situation, a preview might sound like this: "In the next twenty minutes, I will discuss sales in each of three regions: the Southwest, the Far West, and the Midwest." On less formal occasions, your preview might be "I'd like to go over the sales figures in three regions." In any situation, the point of the preview is to give your audience a skeleton, a very general outline, of what you will be discussing.

State your main points clearly. Here are four techniques to apply to oral presentation structure specifically:

1. <u>Follow your preview</u>. After your opening and preview, launch into your main points. Each main point should be exactly the same as each main

point you outlined in your preview; speakers often confuse their listeners by previewing one set of points and then discussing only some of them or adding extras.

2. Limit your main points. Be sure to limit the number of main points you make in a presentation, since listeners cannot process as much information as readers can. Experiments in cognitive psychology show that people cannot easily comprehend more than three to five main points. Naturally, this doesn't mean that you say three things and sit down; it means that you should group your complex ideas into three or five major areas.

3. Use explicit transitions. You need longer, more explicit transitions between major sections or subsections when you are speaking than when your are writing. Listeners do not stay oriented as easily as readers do; they may not remember what you are listing. Instead of using short transitions like "second" or "in addition," use longer transitions, such as "the second recommendation is" or "another benefit of this system is."

4. Provide internal summaries. Finally, use internal summaries to conclude each major section or subsection. Listeners may not remember information they hear only once. Here is an example of an internal summary followed by an explicit transition to the next main section: "Now that we have looked at the three elements of the marketing plan—modifying the promotion program, increasing direct mail, and eliminating the coupon program—let's turn to the financial implications of this plan."

Use an effective closing. Your audience is likely to remember your last words. So don't waste your closing saying something like "Well, that's all I have to say" or "I guess that's about it."

Instead, use a strong, obvious, transition phrase—such as "to summarize" or "in conclusion"—to introduce your closing remarks. One effective closing is to summarize your main points. You may feel as though you're being repetitive, but this kind of reinforcement is extremely effective when explaining or instructing. Another kind of closing is to refer to the rhetorical questions, promise, image, or story you used in your opening. Or you might end with a call to action based on what you have presented, making the "what next?" step explicit. As a final example, you might close by referring to the benefits your audience will gain from following the advice in your presentation.

Excerpted from *Guide to Managerial Communication,* by Mary Munter.
Prentice-Hall, Englewood Cliffs, New Jersey, 1992.

F. ANALYZING WHAT YOU'VE READ

1. The author gives four goals for an effective opening. On a sheet of paper, write down the goals in the order of their importance. Number one should be the most important, number four the least. Be prepared to explain why you ordered them the way you did.

2. Previews can be formal or informal. Write a formal and an informal preview statement for each of the following topics:

    a. The pros and cons (positive and negative aspects) of getting a product out in two months that is not as good as it will be in six months—but beating the competition; or waiting six months and putting out a better product—but taking the chance that the competition will get their product out first.

    b. The pros and cons of opening up a new market in Venezuela or Indonesia.

    c. The pros and cons of downsizing.

    d. Corporate rules for taking a leave of absence for the birth of a child or a death in the family.

3. Limiting the number of main points was one of the main recommendations in Munter's article. How many main points does she suggest and why?

4. Give two additional examples of explicit transitions (different from Munter's).

5. Why is the closing of an oral presentation important?

G. JARGON, BUZZWORDS, AND SLANG: ORAL PRESENTATIONS

1. Circle the best definition or explanation for the underlined terms from Munter's article.

    a. "I feel it is <u>crucial</u> for the president to meet all employees," the human resources officer said.

       interesting

       (important)

       internal

    b. "No one questions Stan's <u>credibility</u>. He's always been honest with us," said Randy.

       You can believe Stan.

       You must doubt Stan.

       You should distrust Stan.

    c. Michael is a <u>competent</u> worker. He is always on the ball and does a good job.

       Michael is a lazy worker.

       Michael is a clumsy worker.

       Michael is a skilled worker.

    d. I made a <u>startling</u> discovery. I found one customer had spent $14,000 on stationery for a company with three employees!

       I made a surprising discovery.

       I made an expected discovery.

       I made an intelligent discovery.

    e. Chris will <u>launch</u> the new product in Chicago on Tuesday.

       Chris will introduce the new product.

       Chris will analyze the new product.

       Chris will finish the new product.

    f. My boss always wants an <u>explicit</u> response.

       My boss always wants a precise response.

       My boss always wants an honest response.

       My boss always wants a gentle response.

2. On a sheet of paper, write your responses to the following:

    a. Write down one crucial thing you must do this week.

    b. Describe one time when you doubted or trusted a stranger's credibility.

IT WORKS!
Learning Strategy:
Associating New
Words with Words
You Already Know

c. Choose one task (e.g., driving a car, or being a tour guide for business executives, or drawing a map of your home town) and explain why you are competent at that job.

d. Name one startling fact about yourself.

e. If you were going to launch your own business, what would it be?

f. In your country, is it polite to explicitly ask a woman her age?

H. PUTTING IT ALL TOGETHER

Following Munter's guidelines, prepare a five-minute oral presentation to give to the company on a business topic of interest to you. It may be a topic that is covered in the chapters in this book, or it may be something different (e.g., the Fortune 500, takeovers, a company to watch, a report on business news from a daily paper, etc.).

I. LISTENING: CONVERSING WITH THE DISABLED

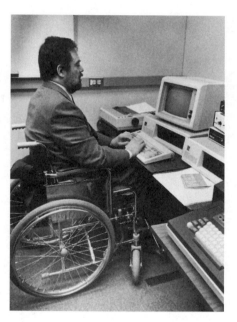

More and more corporations are hiring people with disabilities. Because of this, people need to learn about appropriate topics of conversation with the disabled.

You are going to listen to people with disabilities talk about their ideas on appropriate topics of conversation. Before you listen, discuss the following questions with an associate and write down your answers.

- If a person has a disability, should you ask him or her about it? Why or why not?
- If you meet a couple at a party, and the husband is in a wheelchair, should you ask him or his wife about the disability? Why or why not?
- If a person is visually impaired, should you avoid expressions like "see you later"? Why or why not?

Now listen to what people who have disabilities have to say about the questions you have just answered, and compare your responses to their information.

[Now, listen to the speaker.]

J. PUTTING IT ALL TOGETHER

For one week, look at a newspaper from cover to cover. (You should read any articles that interest you.) Each day when you come to class, spend five minutes walking around and making small talk with your classmates. In that five minutes, introduce two of your classmates to each other. Each time you engage one of them in conversation, bring up an item you read about in the newspaper that day or the previous day.

Evaluation

How well did you achieve the objectives for this chapter? List your results on a sheet of paper. Use the prompts that accompany each objective.

OBJECTIVES	RESULTS
Business 1. To understand the importance of and practice making conversation (including small talk) with an associate, customer, or client in business and social situations 2. To learn how to prepare an oral presentation for a business situation 3. To learn how to introduce a business associate in a social situation 4. To discover what conversation topics are appropriate and inappropriate with a disabled person in business settings **Language** 5. To understand and practice using tag questions **Personal** _____ _____ _____	**Business** 1. Describe two ways you can prepare to make small talk. 2. List three important points about preparing an oral presentation. 3. Making up your own information about them, introduce Ralph Davis to Mary Andrews. 4. List two conversation topics that are appropriate with a disabled person. **Language** 5. Give three examples of tag questions. **Personal** _____ _____ _____

Now answer the following questions:

- What are your strengths in the area of oral communication?
- How can you continue to learn about oral communication on your own?

Written Communication

3

In this chapter, you'll

- learn basic principles of effective business writing.
- recognize effective examples of business writing.
- improve your comprehension of written business communications such as memos and letters.
- practice writing memos and letters.
- understand and use language related to written business communication.

The writer does the most who gives his reader the most knowledge, and takes from him the least time.

—Charles Caleb Colton, c. 1780–1832. English cleric, sportsman, and wine merchant. From *Lacon*.

The average businessperson spends about one-third of his or her time writing memos and letters. And because someone has to read all this writing, businesspeople need to get their messages across as clearly and directly as possible. This chapter introduces you to some basic principles of efficient written communication for business.

PART I

Preparation

A. BRAINSTORMING

With your business team, study the following letter. After you read the letter, answer the questions on a sheet of paper.

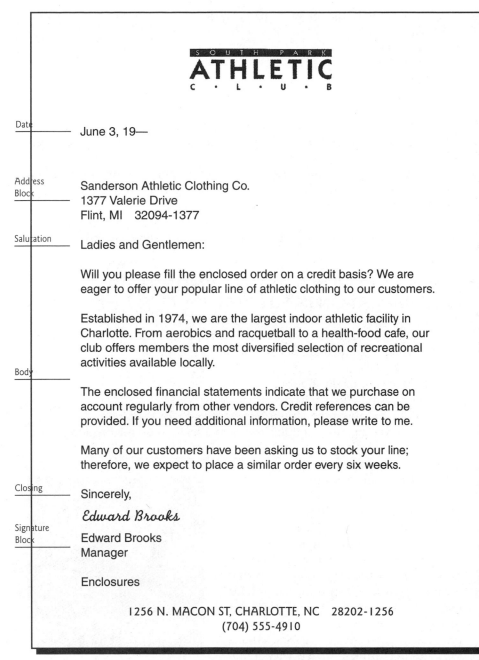

Date

June 3, 19—

Address
Block

Sanderson Athletic Clothing Co.
1377 Valerie Drive
Flint, MI   32094-1377

Salutation

Ladies and Gentlemen:

Body

Will you please fill the enclosed order on a credit basis? We are eager to offer your popular line of athletic clothing to our customers.

Established in 1974, we are the largest indoor athletic facility in Charlotte. From aerobics and racquetball to a health-food cafe, our club offers members the most diversified selection of recreational activities available locally.

The enclosed financial statements indicate that we purchase on account regularly from other vendors. Credit references can be provided. If you need additional information, please write to me.

Many of our customers have been asking us to stock your line; therefore, we expect to place a similar order every six weeks.

Closing

Sincerely,

Edward Brooks

Signature
Block

Edward Brooks
Manager

Enclosures

1256 N. MACON ST, CHARLOTTE, NC   28202-1256
(704) 555-4910

Adapted from *Business Communications,* Tenth Edition, Himstreet, Baty, and Lehman, p. 313. Wadsworth Publishing Company, 1993.

1. Is this a letter from
   a. an athletic clothing manufacturer to an athletic club?
   b. an athletic club to an athletic clothing manufacturer?
   c. an athletic club to an athletic equipment manufacturer?
2. Where is the main idea of the letter stated?
3. What is the purpose of the second paragraph?
4. What is the purpose of the third paragraph?
5. What does the word "Enclosures" mean at the end of the letter?

Threads

In the United States,
a freelance technical
writer can earn
$50–$75 an hour
writing and editing
software documentation
for a large corporation.

6. Give the location of the following parts of the letter:
   • the date
   • the address block
   • the salutation
   • the body of the letter
   • the closing
   • the signature block
     What generalization can you make about the position of these parts?
7. What kind of punctuation did this letter writer use after the salutation? After the closing?
8. This is an example of a business letter that deals with routine or pleasant matters, such as making a request. What are some other types or purposes of business letters?

Now, compare your answers with those of another business team.

B. WORKING WITH CONCEPTS: WRITTEN COMMUNICATION IN BUSINESS

We asked three business people to tell us about the kinds of writing they have to do at work. Read their answers to the following questions:

• What kind of writing do you have to do for your work?
• How much writing do you have to do for your work?
• How do you feel about the writing you have to do for your job?
• How much writing did you think you would have to do for this job before you started it?

1. Sanjiv Ray, analyst/programmer, large manufacturing company: "I have to do a lot of writing. About 50 percent of my time is spent writing. I write memos, letters, and reports, but most of it is documentation—written guidelines on how to use software. I don't feel that great about it, to tell you the truth. It's a chore. Most programmers hate it. What's made it easier is all the new word processing software. Before I started this job, I didn't think I'd have very much writing to do."

2. Sandra Stumbaugh, marketing manager, small food-service company: "About 50 to 60 percent of my time is spent writing. I write memos, ad copy, marketing plans, and press releases. I enjoy writing. People who go into marketing expect to do a lot of writing. Depending on the size of the company, a marketing manager can often delegate writing tasks. But they still need strong writing skills in order to edit other people's work."

3. Jenny Lim, accountant, large telecommunications company: "I do quite a bit of memo writing in my job. A lot of it is situational analysis—keeping others up-to-date on what is happening with a particular project. Writing is also a big part of the business planning process. My group just put out a 150-page five-year-plan report, a kind of project proposal that I helped write and edit. It's very satisfying when the proposal is accepted, but I don't like rewriting it after getting reviewer comments. I didn't think I'd have to do this much writing to be an accountant—in fact, I *didn't* have to at first, but the more responsibility you acquire in this field, the more writing you have to do."

C. JARGON, BUZZWORDS, AND SLANG: TYPES OF BUSINESS WRITING

The business people in Exercise B mention several types of writing that they have to do for their jobs. With an associate, write your own definitions of the following terms on a sheet of paper. Refer to the comments in Exercise B.

Types of Business Writing
ad copy
marketing plan
five-year plan
proposal
documentation
press release
memo

Now, read the following situations and decide what type of writing you would have to do for each one. Fill in the blanks with the type of writing from the preceding list.

1. You work for the marketing department of a food-service company. The company is going to open a new restaurant in a great neighborhood location. You want to tell people in the neighborhood about the new restaurant, so you're going to write ____*ad copy*____ for advertising space you've bought in the neighborhood newspaper.

2. You're the manager of an information resources group in a large corporation. Your group is developing software for another department in the organization. You and some of your team members are going to write

_____ so people will know how to use the software.

3. You've just been hired as the marketing manager for a small software company that has developed a new product. You are going to develop a

_____ that outlines your strategies for introducing, marketing, and advertising the product. This report will include, among other things, descriptions of potential customers, competing products and their prices, the best places to sell the product, and a budget for the entire process.

Threads

The world's largest
public relations
company is Burson
Marsteller, in New York
City. The company had a
net fee income of
$210.372 million in
1990.

Guinness Book of Records, 1993

4. A hospital is looking for an architect to design a new addition. You have a small architecture firm. You and your partners are going to develop a

   _____ that describes your ideas for the new wing. You hope the hospital directors will hire your firm to do the work, based on this document.

5. You work in the human resources department of a medium-sized company. You have hired a consultant to give a seminar designed to help employees

   improve their writing skills. You are going to write a _____ to inform employees of the seminar.

6. You work in the community relations department of a large company that manufactures household products (cleansers, detergents, etc.). The company has just developed a nonpolluting laundry detergent. Because everyone is concerned about the environment, this development improves the company's image. You want as many people to know about this as

   possible, so you write a _____ that you will send to editors at the all the major newspapers around the country. You hope that the newspaper editors will be interested enough in the story to have reporters write articles about your company.

7. You are a manager in the financial planning department of an investment company. Every five years, you and your staff have to write a

   _____ to submit to the vice president of your division. This document outlines a business plan for the future. It outlines how your department plans to increase revenue for the company, and what resources and staff you need in order to implement the plan.

LEARNING STRATEGY

Managing Your Learning: Thinking of your own questions to ask about a topic helps you become an independent learner.

D. PUTTING IT ALL TOGETHER

Interview someone in business. It can be a relative, a friend, a friend of a friend, a neighbor, or one of your teachers. Ask him or her the same questions you saw in Exercise B. You can make up your own questions, too. Ask the person you interview to bring you samples of the kinds of writing he or she does at work.

Write the person's profession here: _____

Before you do your interview:

• Predict the amount of time you think he or she spends writing for his or her job (circle one):

                      0%   10%   30%   50%   75%   90%

- Prepare for the interview by reading the following suggested questions and thinking of some of your own. Write the questions on a sheet of paper; leave room below each one to record the answers from the interview.

1. What kind of writing do you have to do for your work?
2. How much writing do you have to do for your work? (Give a percentage of the total work time.)
3. How do you feel about the writing you have to do for your job?
4. How much writing did you think you would have to do for this job before you started it?
5. Add several questions of your own.

Now, do the interview and record your answers.

LEARNING STRATEGY

Personalizing: Identifying your feelings about a subject makes the subject more meaningful.

E. DEBRIEFING MEETING

In a company meeting, share your interview results from Exercise D and any writing samples you were able to get. As you discuss the answers you received, consider the following:

- What information surprised you the least? The most?
- What kind of writing samples did you get?
- How would you feel if you had to do this type or amount of writing?
- What can you do to prepare for this type or amount of writing?

LEARNING STRATEGY

Managing Your Learning: Setting goals increases your chances for success.

F. SETTING OBJECTIVES

Following are the goals for this chapter. Read them, and consider your personal goals. At the end of this chapter, on page 51, you'll list your results.

OBJECTIVES

Business

1. To learn basic principles of effective business writing
2. To understand the types and amount of writing typical business people in various professions have to do for their jobs
3. To recognize effective examples of business writing, especially memos and letters
4. To improve reading comprehension of business communications textbooks and examples of business letters and memos
5. To practice writing memos and letters

Language

6. To understand and be able to use words and expressions related to the topic of business writing
7. To learn sets of verbs that are always followed by gerunds or infinitives

Personal

_____

_____

_____

PART II

Integration

Threads

The most frequently used words in English, in order of frequency, are: the, of, and, to, a, in, that, is, I, it, for, and as.

Guinness Book of Records, 1993

A. BUSINESS WRITING QUICK AND EASY— SOME GENERAL PRINCIPLES

Writing experts have analyzed what makes memos and business letters easy to read. One expert, Laura Brill, the author of *Business Writing Quick & Easy*, lists ten simple rules to follow. Before you read Brill's advice, do the following task with your business team: List three or more rules you think people should follow when writing business communications.

BUSINESS WRITING QUICK & EASY
by Laura Brill

Here are some simple rules to follow when writing business communications:

1. Write the way you speak. If you wouldn't say something, don't write it. Don't, however, use slang or colloquial expressions.
2. Be as specific and concrete as possible in your choice of language. Avoid abstract, fancy-sounding words and phrases that wouldn't make sense to all your readers.
3. Avoid jargon. If you use it, define terms for your lay audience.
4. Use a friendly, positive tone for letters. Avoid clichés and use phrases that sound businesslike.
5. Get to the point as quickly as possible in all your writing. Don't wait until the middle or end to express your message.
6. Translate archaic language into conversational words and phrases. Say "if" instead of "in the event that" and "give" instead of "render."
7. Use 17 or fewer words per sentence. And if some of your sentences are long (which they certainly can be), balance them with shorter sentences.
8. Read your communications aloud from time to time; you'll pick up inconsistencies and repetition, among other errors.
9. Proofread carefully, preferably at least a few hours after you've written the document. Otherwise you'll get caught up in the majesty of your language and overlook some silly typos.
10. Put yourself in your reader's place. Ask yourself whether the communication would get the job done for you. And remember: There's no substitute for common sense. Apply yours all the time.

Business Writing Quick & Easy, by Laura Brill. AMACON, a division of
American Management Association, New York. 1989. P. 5.

LEARNING STRATEGY

Forming Concepts: Analyzing what you've read helps you understand it better.

B. ANALYZING WHAT YOU'VE READ

With your business team, answer on a sheet of paper the following questions about the passage you just read.

1. Did the author present any of the same rules that you and your associates thought of before you read the selection? What were they?
2. Why should you read your communications aloud before you send them out?
3. Where in a memo or letter should you state your main purpose for writing? Why do you think you should state your main idea in this location?
4. What is "proofreading"? When should you proofread your communications?
5. What is a "typo"? Can you find one in this sentnece?
6. Why is it a good idea to put yourself in your reader's place?

C. JARGON, BUZZWORDS, AND SLANG: BUSINESS LANGUAGE

Following is a list of some types of language to avoid in business writing, according to Brill. Work with an associate. Share your understanding of the language types and match the definitions on the right with the terms on the left.

TERMS: TYPES OF LANGUAGE

___*e*___ slang

_____ colloquial expression

_____ jargon

_____ cliché

_____ archaic language

_____ abstract language

DEFINITIONS

a. Words and expressions used in a particular field of study or profession. People who aren't in the field or profession usually don't know what they mean.

b. Words and expressions that are overused—so much so that they have begun to lose meaning

c. An idiomatic expression used in informal communication. This kind of expression is usually difficult for nonnative speakers to understand.

d. Language that is vague, unclear, or imprecise

e. Words and expressions that are *very* informal

f. Words and expressions that are old-fashioned or no longer in use

NOTE The terms "slang" and "colloquial expression" are very close in meaning.

Now read the following sentences. They contain bad examples of word usage in business communications. The "bad" words and expressions are underlined. Read each sentence and think about what is wrong with the underlined material. Then, using a separate piece of paper, rewrite the sentence. The first sentence is rewritten for you.

1. In a letter to a lay audience—people who don't know very much about educational CD-ROM software for children: "Waldo's Wacky Adventure" brings high quality animation to children's CD-ROM <u>edutainment</u>."
   A better way to say this is:
   <u>"Waldo's Wacky Adventure" educates children while entertaining them</u>.
2. In a memo from a team manager to the vice president of her division: "Project completion will be delayed by two weeks because the software we ordered <u>bombed</u>."
3. In the closing of a letter to an important new client from an electronics company: "<u>Thank you for your patronage</u>."
4. In a letter from an American company to a prospective foreign client: "You'll find that our consultants really know <u>the ins and outs</u> of the business."
5. In a letter responding to a request for information on how to operate a machine: "The <u>logistics</u> of <u>manipulation</u> are really quite simple."
6. In a letter terminating an agreement with a vendor (a supplier of goods and/or services): "Please <u>render</u> all equipment on loan to you by December 31."

D. PUTTING IT ALL TOGETHER

With your business team, read the following letter. Locate these problems:

- wrong placement of the main idea
- a colloquial expression
- a cliché
- one or more typos

Identify any other problems you find. Then rewrite the letter and compare your revision with others at a company meeting.

RACKLEY
ENGINEERING CONSULTANTS

5932 SOUTH SPARTAN ROAD
HACKENSACK, NJ 07602-1700
(201) 555-8134
FAX (201) 555-1234

December 3, 19—

Ms. Barbara Lane, Project Manager
Rackley Engineering Consultants
23, rue de Penthievre
75008 Paris
FRANCE

Dear Ms. Lane:

For the past five years, I have worked as a staff engineer in the Environmental Group at Rackley. Yesterday I received news of my impending tranfser to Paris, France, to work in our plant location there.

I am writing you to ask if you have any advice to help me make my transition to the Paris operation—my first overseas assinment. Because you have been working in the Paris office for the past ten years, I felt you would already know the ropes and could be a great help.

Thanking you in advance,

Sincerely,

Don McClure
Staff Engineer

Adapted from *Business Communications,* Tenth Edition, Himstreet, Baty, & Lehman, p. 323. Wadsworth Publishing Company, 1993.

Communication Memo • Communication Memo • Communication Memo

To: All Employees
From: Corporate Communications Department
Re: Verbs that are followed by gerunds or infinitives

Because gerunds and infinitives often appear in business communications, please review our corporate rules regarding these forms:

Review→   A **gerund** looks like the present participle form of a verb (verb + *ing*), but it's used as a noun. For example:

> **to work→   working→**   I enjoy **working** for Procter & Gamble.

An infinitive is a verb preceded by "to." It is also used as a noun. For example:

> **work→   to work→**   I hope **to work** for Procter & Gamble when I graduate.

Some verbs are always followed by gerunds, some are always followed by infinitives, and some are followed by either. Since there are no rules, you must memorize sets like the following:

Verbs Followed by Gerunds

Here is a list of verbs used in business situations that are *always* followed by gerunds:

spend time	enjoy	recommend	suggest
consider	avoid	be worth	involve

EXAMPLE: A survey showed that many business people <u>spend</u> 30 percent of their <u>time</u> ***writing*** memoranda.

Verbs Followed by Infinitives

Here is a list of verbs used in business situations that are *always* followed by infinitives:

expect	afford	hope	intend
refuse	manage	tend	decide

EXAMPLE: As a marketing manager, <u>I expect</u> ***to do*** a lot of writing at work.

Please fill out the enclosed attachment and return it to your department head.

Enc.

Memo Attachment

Complete the following sentences with either the gerund or infinitive form of the verb in parenthesis:

1. When you write a memo, consider (use) _____*using*_____ bullets at the beginning of each item in a list.

2. Rajiv didn't expect (write) _____ documentation when he first became an analyst/programmer.

3. Accounting professionals tend (do) _____ a lot of writing when they get to higher levels in their organizations.

4. It's a good idea to spend time (proofread) _____ business communications before you send them out.

5. Thank you for your consideration. I hope (have) _____ the chance to work with you in the future.

6. Paul managed (edit) _____ the entire 150-page report over the weekend.

7. A stimulating, highly paid position is worth (wait) _____ for.

8. Would you consider (review) _____ this proposal

E. WRITING MEMORANDA

Most business majors take at least one course in business communication, and they use a textbook written specifically on the subject. You are going to read an excerpt from one of these texts, titled *Advanced Business Communication*.

LEARNING STRATEGY

Forming Concepts: Making predictions about something you are going to read increases your understanding of the material.

Before you read the selection, read this memo from the Maxwell Corporation and discuss with your business team how a memo differs from a letter.

MAXWELL
CORPORATION

TO: All Employees
FROM: Greg Hamlin, Director of Human Resources
DATE: December 15, 19—
SUBJECT: ADDITIONAL VACATION DAY

The board of directors has approved one additional vacation day for every employee.

This decision is our way of expressing gratitude for the most productive and profitable year in the history of the Maxwell Corporation. With the approval of your department head, you may select any day between January 2 and June 30. This day of vacation is in addition to year-end bonuses you will receive soon.

Thank you for all you have done to make the year successful, and best wishes for a healthy and happy new year.

329 SHEPARD ROAD • BELLINGHAM, WA 98225-3983 • (206) 555-4000

Adapted from *Business Communications,* Tenth Edition, Himstreet, Baty, & Lehman, p. 332. Wadsworth Publishing Company, 1993.

Writing memoranda

by Penrose, Rasperry, and Myers

There are a few differences in the organization of memoranda and letters. Memoranda and letters differ somewhat in appearance. *To:* and *From:* replace a letter's inside address and signature block, for example. Further, letters are usually sent outside the organization, while memoranda are usually internal messages. As internal messages, memoranda tend to be more informal and more direct than their letter counterparts.

One survey of 800 business people showed they spent from 21 to 38 percent of their time writing memoranda. There must be a lot of executives overwhelmed by the number of memos they receive! As a result, competition for the reader's time places importance on directness and clarity in memos. So perhaps even more so than with letters, memos should start with a statement of the purpose early in the message. In other words, memos are direct messages— messages that do not contain any extraneous information.

Memoranda also need special visual treatment. Keep paragraphs short, much like newspaper articles. Consider using bullets (asterisks, lowercase *o*'s, or large dots) in front of items in a list. A recent approach to typing memoranda— probably enhanced by software packages and computers—places the main text of the memo in a narrow column and then, to the left of it, adds notes summarizing the contents. In the last several years, college textbook designers have learned that readers prefer this approach for its ease of understanding, organizational clarity, and speed of review. These same attributes hold true for memoranda preparation. An example appears on page 46.

Computers increasingly aid mid- and upper-level managers who prepare their own memos without secretarial help. If you prepare your own correspondence, realize the importance of dating your messages. Knowing precisely when you recommended, ordered, signed, or asked about something often is crucial. Computers often can date (or time-stamp) information for you easily.

Another characteristic that can set memoranda apart from letters is the inclusion of humor. Humor—or attempts at it—require judicious use in both memos and letters. However, when the internal message is lighthearted and relatively unimportant, humor in a memo can distinguish its author as a person with personality and depth. As long as the humor is on target, does not embarrass others, is not overdone, and is not too frequent, it can reflect positively on its author. A word of caution is needed, however; what is funny to you may not be funny to others. You may wish to test your message on a neutral friend.

Threads

Copying software illegally is a federal crime with fines of up to $100,000.

MEMO

To: Regional Managers
From: Fred Gilley, Vice President, Planning
Subject: Improving Regional Meetings
Date: December 3, 199X

Managers, I have a few thoughts for you:

AMENITIES AT MEETINGS

One of the objectives of regional meetings should be to provide opportunities for attendees to meet and talk with one another. Our decentralized organization does not lend itself to intraregional communications. Therefore, we should make the most of our regional meetings by providing the following:

- a reception for everyone the night we arrive
- a luncheon for everyone on Friday
- a reception for VIPs and speakers on Friday night
- coffee midmorning Friday and Saturday
- coffee and soft drinks midafternoon Friday.

Minimal cost is involved in providing these amenities and they provide the occasions for informal visits.

JOINT MEETINGS

Last year the Southwest region and the Southeast region met in New Orleans for a joint meeting. The regions shared common discussion for the first day and then split into their respective groups for the next two days for topics relevant only to themselves.

Those in attendance agree the sessions were valuable and that it was enjoyable interacting with those from another region. Maybe other regions should consider having joint meetings.

Adapted from *Advanced Business Communication,* by Penrose, Rasberry, and Myers, pp. 162–166. Wadsworth Publishing Company, 1993.

F. ANALYZING WHAT YOU'VE READ

On a sheet of paper, answer these questions about the material on memos that you just read.

1. What are three ways that memos and letters differ?
2. Why should memos be direct?
3. What are bullets, and why would you use them in a memo?
4. Why should you be careful about using humor in memos?

LEARNING STRATEGY

Forming Concepts: Applying new information to a realistic situation helps you understand it better.

---

5. Decide whether to send a memo or a letter for each of the following situations. Circle "Memo" or "Letter" to indicate your choice.
   a. You are a manager. You want to inform your group of the agenda for an upcoming project status meeting.
   Memo   Letter
   b. You work for Beta Software, Inc. You met a potential customer at a recent computer show. You want to remind this person that you met, and tell her a little more about your products.
   Memo   Letter
   c. You are writing a 150-page five-year plan for your department. You need to tell someone in the desktop publishing department at your company about a design change in the document.
   Memo   Letter

G. JARGON, BUZZWORDS, AND SLANG: MEMO TALK

Match the following terms from the excerpt on memos with the definitions and synonyms on the right.

extraneous	Another word for "company"
memoranda	Something that you communicate
message	Another word for "memo"
visual	Inside an organization, rather than outside
organization	A memo that has this is easy to understand
internal	Something that is extra, or not necessary
clarity	This makes an item in a list easier to read
bullet	Having to do with the way something looks

Now, locate each of the terms on the left in the word search puzzle that follows. The words can appear horizontally, vertically, or diagonally. They can also appear forwards or backwards.

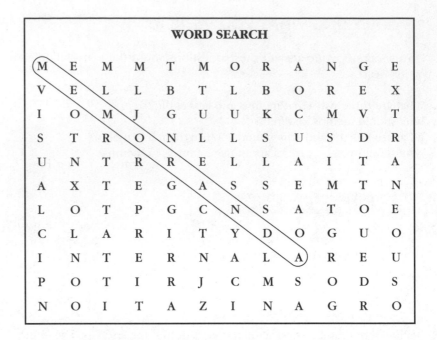

WORD SEARCH

```
M  E  M  M  T  M  O  R  A  N  G  E
V  E  L  L  B  T  L  B  O  R  E  X
I  O  M  J  G  U  U  K  C  M  V  T
S  T  R  O  N  L  L  S  U  S  D  R
U  N  T  R  R  E  L  L  A  I  T  A
A  X  T  E  G  A  S  S  E  M  T  N
L  O  T  P  G  C  N  S  A  T  O  E
C  L  A  R  I  T  Y  D  O  G  U  O
I  N  T  E  R  N  A  L  A  R  E  U
P  O  T  I  R  J  C  M  S  O  D  S
N  O  I  T  A  Z  I  N  A  G  R  O
```

H. PUTTING IT ALL TOGETHER

Working with an associate, practice writing memos for particular business situations. Follow these steps:

1. Choose one of the following situations.
2. Write an appropriate memo and send it to your associate. (Indicate in the memo that you need a response.)
3. Then write a memo in response to the one you received.

Situations

1. You are a manager at a software company. You are scheduling visits to Value Added Resellers—companies that create and sell a product that incorporates *your* product. Write a memo asking an employee you manage to give you three dates in the next month when it would be convenient for him or her to make this five-day business trip.
2. Your company has a community involvement program—a program in which employees do volunteer projects in the community, on company time. You are helping a middle school in the neighborhood, and you want your co-workers to join you. Write a memo encouraging their participation, and suggest ways in which they might be of help. Some possibilities might be:
   • help set up a computer lab
   • tutor math, English, or science
   • donate computers or office equipment
   • give a talk on Career Day
   • (your ideas)
3. Write a memo asking your associate for an evaluation of the meeting with the person he or she interviewed in Part 1, Exercise D, p. 36.
4. Write a memo about your own situation.

Now, choose a new situation and repeat Steps 1–3.

I. LISTENING: THE VALUE OF WRITTEN REPORTS

You are going to hear a recorded excerpt from *The Wall Street Journal on Management: The Best of the Manager's Journal.* The *Manager's Journal* is a weekly column appearing in the *Wall Street Journal.* (For more information about the *Wall Street Journal,* see Chapter 7.) The column provides practical advice about real-life challenges typical managers face.

Listen to the selection once. Listen for the answer to this question:

- According to the speaker, which is more important, *writing* reports or *reading* reports?

[Now, listen to the speaker.]

Now, listen again and circle the correct answers to the following questions.

HINT Read the questions before you listen.

1. How do most managers get information?
   in written form   in conversational exchanges
2. Does the speaker think written reports provide timely information?
   Yes   No

Now listen to the recording again, as many times as you want, and answer these questions:

- Why is writing a report such an important activity, according to the speaker?
- Do you agree or disagree? Why?

J. PUTTING IT ALL TOGETHER

You are going to conduct an information interview. An information interview involves talking to someone who has the kind of position or profession you would like to have. You ask this person questions about what he or she does and how he or she got her job. The interview should take no more than 20 minutes. Work with a business team of associates who have career goals similar to yours, and follow these steps:

1. Identify contacts—people to interview. You can either interview the same person you interviewed in Part I, Exercise D (a relative, friend, etc.), or find someone new. Get the person's name, title, company, phone number, and address.
2. Call to make an appointment. Make sure you state that you are requesting an information interview only and that it will take 20 minutes or less.
3. Optional: Write a letter to your contact confirming your interview appointment. If you don't write this letter, call the morning of the interview to confirm your appointment.
4. Write a memo to your business team describing your contact and what you plan to ask him or her. Consider asking how much writing he or she does.

5. With your business team, take turns role-playing your interview. Evaluate one anothers' interviews using the following chart. Check whether you thought your associates' form, tone, and nonverbal behavior were appropriate or inappropriate. Then give comments and suggestions to your associates for each feature.

Associate A (interviewer)

FEATURE	APPROPRIATE	INAPPROPRIATE	COMMENTS AND SUGGESTIONS
Form			
Tone			
Nonverbal behavior			

Associate B (contact)

FEATURE	APPROPRIATE	INAPPROPRIATE	COMMENTS AND SUGGESTIONS
Form			
Tone			
Nonverbal behavior			

6. Go to your appointment. Take notes. Watch the time. At the end of the interview, ask your contact for the names of other people who might be willing to talk to you. Don't forget to thank your contact.
7. Write a thank-you note to your contact thanking him or her for seeing you.
8. Write a memo to your business team summarizing what you learned from your information interview.

   NOTE Allow plenty of time for this assignment!

When everyone on your business team has had the interview, and you've written and received your summary memos, hold a short meeting to discuss how well you think the project went and what you would do differently next time.

Evaluation

How well did you achieve the objectives for this chapter? List your results on a sheet of paper. Use the prompts that accompany each objective.

OBJECTIVES	RESULTS
Business **1.** To learn basic principles of effective business writing **2.** To understand the types and amount of writing typical business people in various professions have to do for their jobs **3.** To recognize effective examples of business writing, especially memos and letters **4.** To improve reading comprehension of business communications textbooks and examples of business letters and memos **5.** To practice writing memos and letters	**Business** **1.** List one or more basic principles of business writing. **2.** Give examples of two types of writing business people have to do. **3.** Look again at the letter in Part II, Exercise D, p. 41. Explain one thing that is wrong with it. **4.** Tell one thing you learned about memos from the excerpt "Writing Memoranda," Part II, Exercise E., p. 43. **5.** Write one thing you learned from the letter- and memo-writing you did in Part II, Exercise H (Putting It All Together), p. 48.
Language **6.** To understand and be able to use words and expressions related to the topic of business writing **7.** To learn sets of verbs that are always followed by gerunds or infinitives	**Language** **6.** Write a sentence using one or more new buzzwords or expressions you learned in this chapter. **7.** Write a sentence about business communication using a verb + gerund construction. Then write a sentence about business communication using a verb + infinitive construction.
Personal _____ _____ _____	**Personal** _____ _____ _____

Now answer the following questions:

• What are your strengths in the area of written business communication?
• How can you continue to learn about written business communication on your own?

Corporate Culture

CHAPTER PREVIEW

In this chapter, you'll

- learn about corporate culture.
- discover the features the best companies share.
- practice presentation skills.
- express your understanding of corporate culture through writing.

> *When I am in Milan, I do as they do in Milan; but when I go to Rome, I do as Rome does.*
>
> —St. Augustine (A.D. 345–430), quoting St. Ambrose

Corporate culture is a major factor in how well people get along in their work environment. In this chapter, you'll look at corporate culture in several companies and discover what the best companies to work for have in common.

PART I

Preparation

A. BRAINSTORMING

On a sheet of paper, answer the following questions on your own. Then discuss your answers with your business team.

LEARNING STRATEGY

Forming Concepts: Defining terms can help you clarify your thinking, which in turn can help you become a better speaker and writer.

1. What groups fit the term "corporation"?
2. What does the term "culture" mean?
3. How would you define the term "corporate culture"?
4. Look at the picture of the office reception area in the chapter opener, on page 53. Would you like to work there? Why?

B. WORKING WITH CONCEPTS: MAJOR CHANGES IN CORPORATE CULTURE FROM THE 1980S TO THE 1990S

In 1984, Levering and Moskowitz wrote a book called *The Hundred Best Companies to Work for in America*. In 1993, they updated that book. Read the following excerpt from their introduction to the latest edition, in which they talk about the differences between what they saw in the 1980s and what they see in the 1990s. After you read, fill in the grid to check your understanding.

Threads

Percent of Americans who believe their occupation is fulfilling or exciting: 67.

The hundred best companies to work for

by Robert Levering and Milton Moskowitz

We have noted positive change in five key areas: **More employee participation.** A rarity in the early 1980s, genuine employee involvement in decision making about their jobs is a reality among the companies in this book. This change has often occurred because of layoffs. With fewer supervisors, many companies have been forced to recognize how work is accomplished. In some cases, the quality movement—the current management buzzword—has provided specific techniques for increasing employee participation.

More sensitivity to work/family issues. Many of the companies in this book have made tremendous strides toward dealing with the problems of working mothers and fathers, offering a variety of child-care options and flexible work schedules.

More sharing of the wealth. Profit-sharing and gain-sharing programs have increased dramatically, as have ESOPs (employee stock ownership plans). More and more companies are extending stock options, typically reserved for a handful of top executives, to everyone in the ranks.

More fun. Today we see companies where having fun seems to be part of the corporate mission. Fun is not inconsistent with operating a serious, profit-making business. Watch out for companies where there is no sense of humor.

More trust between management and employees. This is a more fundamental characteristic of the new workplace style than quality teams, flex-time or profit-sharing plans. In the best workplaces, employees trust their managers, and the managers trust their employees. The trust is reflected in numerous ways: no time clocks, meetings where employees have a chance to register their concerns, job posting (so that employees have first crack at openings), constant training (so that employees can learn skills), and employee committees empowered to make changes in policies, recommend new pay rates, or allocate the corporate charity dollars. Trust, in the workplace, simply means that employees are treated as partners and recognized as having something to contribute beyond brawn or manual dexterity or strong legs and arms.

There is more trust today because the authoritarian work-style that has long been the standard operating procedure in American business has failed. It hasn't worked for employees, and it hasn't worked for employers. And that failure is at the

root of the poor performance of American companies and the massive layoffs of the late 1980s and early 1990s. When management becomes disconnected from the people who work in the company, it becomes easy to fire them. And when workers are disconnected from what they are doing, it becomes easy for them not to care about the product or service they're delivering.

This failure has impelled companies to look for other options. It is our hope that by providing these concrete examples, employees and employers alike will see that this new work-style is not only possible but realistic and practical. This is true whether your company is big or small, old or young, high-tech or no-tech. The new work-style reflected in this book may be a harbinger of the American workplace in the next century.

The 100 Best Companies to Work for in America, by Robert Levering and Milton Moskowitz, New York: Doubleday, 1993.

With an associate, fill in the blanks in the following chart with your own ideas of specific examples of an 1980s company and a 1990s company:

	1980s COMPANY	1990s COMPANY
employee participation		
sensitivity to work/family issues	_____	_____
sharing of the wealth	_____	_____
fun	_____	_____
trust between management and employees	*time clock punched*	*flex time*

C. BUZZWORDS, JARGON, AND SLANG: CORPORATE CULTURE

Test your understanding of the underlined works and expressions by writing the answers to the following questions on a sheet of paper.

1. Are <u>layoffs</u> good news or bad news for the economy of a country? Why?
2. Does the <u>quality movement</u> lead to more employee involvement or less employee involvement? Why?
3. Would you prefer a <u>flexible work schedule</u> or a rigid work schedule? Why?
4. Would you rather work for a company that has a <u>profit-sharing program</u> or one that does not? Why?
5. Would you rather work for a company that provides <u>ESOPs</u> or one that does not? Why?
6. Would you rather work with someone who has an <u>authoritarian work-style</u> or someone who has an easygoing work-style? Why?

D. PUTTING IT ALL TOGETHER

1. The keyword for each of the differences between the 1980s and the 1990s that Levering and Moskowitz found is "more." If you wanted to apply **more** of all the points mentioned in *The 100 Best Companies to Work for in America* to your daily life, how would you do it? Answer the questions on a sheet of paper.

Personalizing: Relating new concepts to your personal life makes them more meaningful.

    a. How can you have more control over the decisions about your life made by others (e.g., teachers or parents, or others who have control over your life)?

    b. How would you show more sensitivity to work and/or family issues?

    c. How would you share your wealth more? (This could be actual money, but it also could be time, ideas, or other kinds of wealth you may have.)

    d. How could you have more fun in your everyday life?

    e. How could you develop more trust with your friends? Do you think that this would work with management and employees? Why or why not?

2. Now, on your own, or with an associate, go to the library and look for an article about corporate culture written between 1980 and 1985. Then look for an article on corporate culture written within the last two years. Compare the two articles. To find articles, use the *Reader's Guide to Periodical Literature,* or one of the computer guides, such as *InfoTrak.*

E. DEBRIEFING MEETING

In a business team, report on the article you found in Exercise D.

F. SETTING OBJECTIVES

Following are the goals for this chapter. Read them, and consider your personal goals for this chapter. At the end of this chapter, on page 67, you'll list your results.

OBJECTIVES

Business
    1. To learn about corporate culture
    2. To discover the features the best companies share

Language
    3. To practice presentation skills
    4. To express your understanding of corporate culture through writing
    5. To understand and practice expressions of comparison in English

Personal

_____

_____

_____

Threads

Average number of jobs an American worker has held by age 40: 8.

Runzheimer International

Integration

A. A COMPARISON OF TWO CORPORATE CULTURES

You are going to hear a woman—an immigrant to the U.S.—talk about two jobs she has had. Before you listen, do the following two activities to focus your listening:

> ### LEARNING STRATEGY
>
> **Forming Concepts: Thinking about something familiar and similar to a topic you are going to hear helps you focus on the new information.**

1. Think of a company you know something about. Jot down some notes on a sheet of paper about these aspects of the company:
    Name of the company
    a. Pay/benefits
    b. Opportunities to get ahead in the company
    c. Job security
    d. Pride in work/company
    e. Openness/fairness (How much do people inside the company know about what is going on in the company? How fair is the company to women and minorities?)
    f. Camaraderie/friendliness (How friendly are people in the company?)
    g. How would you rate the company you described? Circle your choice.
        excellent   good   fair   poor
    h. Would you like to work for that company? Why or why not?

Communication Memo • Communication Memo • Communication Memo

To: All Employees
From: Corporate Communications Department
Re: Comparison structure in English

Since comparative structures are useful when discussing different corporate cultures, review the following on the use of comparisons:

• With one-syllable words, use:
-er for two items

EXAMPLE The salaries at my new company are <u>higher</u> than at my last company.

-est for three or more items

EXAMPLE The salaries are generally <u>highest</u> in established companies.

• With words of two or more syllables, use:
<u>more</u> for two items

EXAMPLE Your company is <u>more</u> open to new ideas than mine.

<u>the most</u> for three or more items

EXAMPLE I find that new companies are <u>the most</u> open to new ideas.

Please fill out the attached comparison exercise, and check your answers with an associate or your CEO.

GD\ew
Enc.

Memo Attachment

Complete the following sentences, using the correct comparative form.

1. Toys Plus Inc. provides _____*more*_____ benefits than Toys Today Inc. My Toys Inc. provides _____ benefits of the three.

2. Toys Today Inc. has _____ buildings than Toys Plus Inc.

3. Toys Today Inc. has _____ employees of the three companies.

4. The sales force of Toys Plus is _____ (small) than that of My Toys Inc.

5. The pay at My Toys Inc. is _____ (high) than at Toys Today Inc.

2. Test your hypotheses: In the chart below, write your ideas about the differences between working at a big company and a small one for the categories listed:

	BIG COMPANY	SMALL COMPANY
pay benefits	*higher*	
opportunities to get ahead in the company		
job security		
pride in work/in the company		
openness/fairness		
camaraderie/friendliness		*better*

Compare your answers with an associate. Make a list on the board of the areas where you disagreed.

Now listen to Alicia Gomez talking about her experiences at two companies and see how your guesses compare with her answers. After you listen once, read the following questions. Then listen again and, on a sheet of paper, answer the questions. You may want to listen to the tape several times to complete your answers.

[Now, listen to the speaker.]

a. Which items did you and Alicia agree on?
b. Which items were different?
c. How were they different?

B. THE READER'S DIGEST—THEN AND NOW

You are going to read an excerpt from the Robert Levering and Milton Moskowitz book, *The 100 Best Companies to Work for in America,* about one of the best companies in their study, The Reader's Digest.

LEARNING STRATEGY

Forming Concepts: Listing what you already know about a subject before you read about it makes the reading task easier.

Before you read, write out on a sheet of paper what you already know about the *Reader's Digest* magazine and then answer the following questions.

1. Given what you know about the *Reader's Digest* magazine, what kind of a company do you think it is? Do you think it has an authoritarian management style or an easygoing one?

2. What kind of art do you think would be on the walls?
3. What do you think the mission of the magazine is?
4. Do you think it is a family-run company or a corporate-run company?

Compare your list with an associate's.

The Reader's Digest

by Robert Levering and Milton Moskowitz

Shortly after he took over the Reader's Digest Association in 1984, George Grune unlocked the company's boardroom and announced that the room was now open to employees. It was a symbolic act, indicating that under Grune's leadership, the Reader's Digest was going to be different from the genteel, paternalistic place we described in our last edition. True to his word, Grune has shaken up the culture here.

To get an idea of the culture we're talking about, consider the boardroom Grune opened up. It has artworks that any museum in the world would covet—paintings by Renoir, Degas (*Dancers*), Cezanne, Manet, Matisse. Monet (*Water Lilies*), and a sculpture by Picasso. The boardroom is not unique. Reader's Digest's headquarters in Pleasantville, 40 miles north of New York City, houses some 3,000 works of art. The main building is topped with a Georgian tower with four sculptures of the mythical winged horse Pegasus, the Digest's corporate logo. It sits on 127 acres of well-manicured lawns. (The fall day we were there, workers were vacuuming up the leaves that had fallen the night before.) You have the sense of entering a quiet museum rather than a busy magazine office as you spot two Modigliani paintings. Chagall's *The Three Candles* hangs above the desk of the editor in chief of *Reader's Digest,* the flagship magazine of this global media empire.

The editor's office used to be occupied by founder DeWitt Wallace, who, along with his wife, Lila Acheson Wallace, launched *Reader's Digest* in 1922 with condensed articles from other publications. It has become the world's most widely read magazine, selling 28 million copies each month in 17 languages and 41 different editions. Since its humble origins beneath a Greenwich Village speakeasy, the company has become a major book publisher (20 million copies of its Condensed Books in 10 languages are sold annually), CD and record distributor (5 million music collections), and home video seller (1.7 million). And they publish a handful of other magazines: *American Health, The Family Handyman, Moneywise, New Choices for the Best Years,* and *Travel Holiday.*

The Wallaces, both children of ministers, had a clearly defined formula for their "Little Magazine" as *Reader's Digest* was originally subtitled. Articles were to be short, readable, and uplifting ("the best-edited magazine in America"). Subjects were picked to inspire or entertain. Ken Gordon, international group president, told us that the *Digest's* mission, then and now, is to show "the power of the individual to make a difference." The Wallaces didn't accept advertising in the U.S. edition until 1955, and even then they didn't allow any ads for cigarettes, liquor, drugs, or other products they found distasteful.

The Wallaces also had a clear sense of the kind of workplace they wanted. It started as a mom-and-pop operation, and the childless Wallaces always considered employees to be part of their family. Employees still tell stories of how the Wallaces would take care of employees who had met with misfortunes. And they showered their employees with unusual benefits, like a turkey at Thanksgiving, Fridays off in May, four weeks of vacation after only one year on the job, and buses that brought employees to and from work at a cost of $3 a week.

This cozy workplace no longer exists here. The Wallaces both died in their 90s in the early 1980s (DeWitt in 1981, Lila in 1984). George Grune, a former ad salesman who joined the Digest in 1960, has his eye riveted on the bottom line. In a few short years, he turned Reader's Digest on its head. He laid off several hundred workers. Especially hard hit were the blue- and pink-collar departments, such as subscription fulfillment. Reader's Digest continues to hire for more professional positions, however. When we visited in late 1991, there were 100 openings.

* * *

Some employees question whether the drastic changes of the Grune era have destroyed too much of the Wallace culture. Chris Madera, test processing supervisor, said: "Even though we're a tightly knit company, I don't think we feel that we are a family-run company anymore. I think we're more on the corporate level and the competitive level. There is more professionalism in the company, a lot of expectations in all areas, always being aware of cost expenditures. It's no longer family like it was when the Wallaces were alive." Administrative assistant Natasha Cherney added: "I think that kind of personal, paternalistic caring has changed radically. There used to be an intimacy here that is now waning. It's not gone, but it's waning."

Excerpted from The 100 Best Companies to Work for in America, by Robert Levering and Milton Moskowitz. New York: Doubleday, 1993. (pp. 385–387).

Threads

Excellent firms don't
believe in excellence,
only in constant
improvement and
constant change.

Tom Peters, *The Washington Post*, 10/4/87.

C. ANALYZING WHAT YOU'VE READ

Now that you've read the passage, answer the following questions on a sheet of paper. Then compare your answers with the ones you wrote on pp. 60–61.

1. What kind of a company is the Reader's Digest?
2. Does it have an authoritarian management style, or an easygoing one?
3. What kind of art do you think would be on the walls?
4. What is the mission of the magazine?
5. Is it a family-run company or a corporate-run company?

D. JARGON, BUZZWORDS, AND SLANG: TALK AT THE DIGEST

Review this list of expressions from the passage on The Reader's Digest. Then fill in the blanks in the sentences that follow with the appropriate expression from the list.

Expressions

mom-and-pop operation	blue-collar department
bottom line	pink-collar department
turned it on its head	

Now, fill in the blanks with one of the items from the list:

1. When Steve took over the department, he made several major changes—in fact, he really _____.

2. Susan and her husband started their business together. In the beginning the company was just a _____.

3. When she began her business, Susan had to watch the budget carefully. She didn't want to spend more money than the company made, so she kept her eye on the _____.

4. Paul wears a blue work shirt and bluejeans to work in packaging. Packaging is a _____.

5. Sandy works in the food service division of her company. All workers are required to wear light-weight pink jackets. She works in a

_____.

E. PUTTING IT ALL TOGETHER: SMALL TALK AT THE DIGEST

Small talk (see Chapter 1) is important in many business situations, such as before a meeting starts, during a coffee break at a meeting, before and after a job interview, in the hall, or at the water cooler anytime during the day. One topic that comes up in conversation is art, especially when a company has spent some effort and money to have art in public areas. Most Americans have learned about the French Impressionists in college, or even earlier.

Do the following activities to increase your knowledge of art:

• Look up in a newspaper index under "Art" and find out what an Impressionist painting sold for recently. Report on your findings in a company meeting.

- Go to a modern art museum and find the Impressionist paintings there. Describe your findings in a company meeting.
- You and an associate have unlimited money to buy a Monet, Renoir, or Chagall. Decide on a painting and explain to the company why you chose the painting you did. Along with personal taste, you may wish to consider resale value.

F. HONDA OF AMERICA

You are going to read another article from Levering and Moskowitz's book— this time on Honda of America. Before you read the passage, write out on a sheet of paper what you already know about the Honda car and then the answers to the following questions.

1. Given what you know about Hondas, what kind of a company do you think it is? Do you think it has an authoritarian management style or an easygoing one?
2. Honda believes in education for its employees. What kinds of things do you imagine Honda could do to educate employees?

Compare your comments with those of an associate.

Honda of America

by Robert Levering and Milton Moskowitz

Honda introduces its distinctive philosophy, called the Honda Way, to new associates and their family members at an orientation session led by the president of Honda of America (HAM), Hiroyuki Yoshino. After Yoshino and the vice president of human relations, Don English, finish their presentations and answer questions, each new associate introduces himself or herself to their guest, and the executives personally welcome each one to the Honda family. Yoshino is one of 320 Japanese associates working in America, most of them assigned to the R&D [research and development] centers in Marysville and Torrance, California.

Education is a key part of the Honda Way. A training facility offers over 300 different classes, most of them taught by Honda employees. Outside production associates spend an average of 35 hours in the classroom. Honda also sends associates to Japan for training in Honda manufacturing. In 1990, 400 team leaders went to Japan for 4 weeks. Every year about 15 welders and 50 assembly workers go to Honda's Japanese plants. Since 1979 Honda of America has sent more than 3,200 associates to Japan for training.

Honda emphasizes training because it promotes from within. Corporate communications manager Roger Lambert told us: "All but one of the managers in the Marysville auto plant started from the line, so there's quite a bit of opportunity for growth and development and promotion."

Like other Japanese manufacturers, Honda promotes an egalitarian atmosphere. There are no reserved parking spaces or executive dining rooms. Managers and engineers spend their days on the production floor because the Honda Way teaches managers that they must get close to problems to solve them. Desks of managers, engineers, and production staff are located in plain sight on the production floor, while plant managers' offices are just outside the doorways to the shop floor.

The accessibility of managers and executives makes communication easy, according to production associate Johnna Haughn: "In other places, I had a fear of some of my bosses. But that's not the way it is here at Honda. It's all teamwork. Management will dig right in there with you and help solve problems. They're not going to stand back and tell you what to do."

Honda's team atmosphere encourages employees to feel involved in their work. Donnie McGhee started

as a production worker and is now associate relations manager at the Anna engine plant. He explained: "It was mindboggling for me to come here and see the amount of involvement of the general associate in problems and situations that before I viewed only as management-type issues. There is sharing of responsibility. Here is the manager, but right alongside that manager you'll find a general associate. They're both out there, getting their hands dirty, problem solving. Often it's difficult to make that separation between who is the manager and who is the general associate. There is not the divisiveness in this company that I experienced for 15 years at General Motors."

Perry Paynbe, who works at the associate development center, previously worked as a manager for General Motors before coming to the Marysville auto plant in 1984. "I had to make one hell of an adjustment [from GM]," he said. "I was used to that power where you did not allow the employee to get involved. It's shared information here. Initially, it felt like I was losing control."

Excerpted from The 100 Best Companies to Work for in America, by Robert Levering and Milton Moskowitz. New York: Doubleday, 1993. pp. 187–189.

G. JARGON, BUZZWORDS, AND SLANG: HONDA TALK

Review this list of expressions from the passage on Honda of America. Then fill in the blanks in the sentences that follow with the appropriate expression from the list.

Expressions:
mindboggling
the Honda Way
promotion from within
(to) dig right in
(to) stand back
one hell of an adjustment

Now fill in the blanks with one of the expressions from the list:

1. I'd rather _____ than _____. I like to see how things are going before I get involved.
2. When you go to a new country or a new company, you almost always have

   to make _____.

3. It's _____ the way things can change quickly when a company has a new ambitious, effective president.

4. I want to work for a company where there is _____ because I like the idea of moving up in a company.

5. The philosophy of keeping everyone working together at Honda is part

   of _____.

H. ANALYZING WHAT YOU'VE READ

Discuss with an associate the following questions about the passage you just read. Write your answers on a sheet of paper.

1. What do you think about Honda's management style now? Is it an easygoing or authoritarian one? What in the reading tells you how the Honda employees view the management style at Honda?
2. What do you think are the advantages of working for Honda?
3. Based on your reading of the passage, what would be disadvantages of working for Honda?

I. PUTTING IT ALL TOGETHER

LEARNING STRATEGY

Remembering New Material: Using what you've learned in new situations helps you remember it better.

The following activities will help you integrate what you have learned about corporate culture with your previous learning.

1. Call three or four companies in your area. Talk to the human relations person or to someone in personnel and find out what opportunities there are for education at those companies. Report your findings to your business team or in a company meeting.

2. In your business team, design a series of educational courses for a company of your choice. First, describe the company, including what it produces or what service it provides. Give information on the size of the company and the management style. Then list the series of courses. In turn, have each team interview the other teams to find out about the educational programs offered. Write a brief memo to your CEO recommending one of the companies because of the educational opportunities it offers.

3. Choose a company, as you did for Activity 2. Plan and hold an orientation meeting for new employees. Choose a president, a vice president of human relations, and four or five new associates to introduce themselves to the guests. Personally welcome each guest to your company's family. Then describe the corporate culture of the company. Next, switch roles and have the former president, vice president of human relations, and associates be guests. Choose a new president, new vice president of human relations, and new associates, and hold another orientation meeting.

Using the following charts, evaluate how the president and vice president of human relations communicated. Check whether you thought your associates' form, tone, and nonverbal behavior were appropriate or inappropriate. Then give comments and suggestions to your associates for each feature.

The President

FEATURE	APPROPRIATE	INAPPROPRIATE	COMMENTS AND SUGGESTIONS
Form			
Tone			
Nonverbal behavior			

The Vice President

FEATURE	APPROPRIATE	INAPPROPRIATE	COMMENTS AND SUGGESTIONS
Form			
Tone			
Nonverbal behavior			

4. Find a biography of the Wallaces or someone who has started a mom-and-pop company that was successful. (The librarian can help you find an interesting story.) Report on what you learned.

Managing Your Learning: Learning to "read"—analyze—a culture will help you in any new environment.

5. Create personal examples and practice "reading" a culture by answering the following questions individually or with one or two associates:
   • At the Reader's Digest, the artwork on the walls was a visual indication of the corporate culture. What do you think the valuable artwork says about the company?
   • What else would you look at to read a corporate culture? Make a list of points that you could use to learn about a corporate culture.
   • Choose a company that you can visit. Look at the outside of the building. What can you learn about corporate culture from the outside of a building?
   • Looking at the inside of the building, what can you tell about the corporate culture of the corporation located there?

6. Choose two business buildings to look at. You can choose businesses you have not seen (e.g., from the yellow pages of the phone book), or you can choose two business buildings you have seen. Go to the buildings and take notes on the following:
   • How would you describe the outside structure?
   • What material is the building made of?
   • Are there a lot of windows?
   • Are the outside doors large?
   • What do you like about the buildings?
   • What do you dislike about the buildings?
   • Would you like to go to work in the buildings?
        If possible, go inside the buildings, look around, and answer these questions:
   • How close are offices to one another?
   • What colors are the walls?
   • What kind of pictures are on the walls?

Present your findings on the buildings to your business team. First, describe the two buildings. Then tell your associates what companies you visited. Let them guess which building belongs to which company.

Evaluation

How well did you achieve the objectives for this chapter? List your results on a sheet of paper. Use the prompts that accompany each objective.

OBJECTIVES	RESULTS
Business 1. To learn about corporate culture 2. To discover the features the best companies share	**Business** 1. Write a definition of "corporate culture." 2. Describe three characteristics that make a company fit in the category of "best" companies.
Language 3. To practice presentation skills 4. To express your understanding of corporate culture through writing 5. To understand and practice expressions of comparison in Engligh	**Language** 3. Imagine the ideal company to work for. Give a two-minute presentation about how "your" company belongs in the category of "best." 4. Design a letterhead and write a brief memo about the dress code for the ideal corporation you described in Item 3. 5. Write three sentences comparing any two companies regarding pay, job security, and one other characteristic.
Personal _____ _____ _____	**Personal** _____ _____ _____

Now answer the following questions:

- What are your strengths in analyzing corporate culture?
- How can you continue to learn about corporate culture on your own?

Management

In this chapter, you'll

- learn about different management styles, including cultural differences in management styles.
- understand the challenges facing managers in the multicultural workplace.
- select a management style for a project, use it, and then evaluate its effectiveness.
- practice coming to a consensus.
- understand and be able to use words and expressions related to the topic of management.

> *To lead the people, walk behind them.*
>
> —Lao-Tzu, c. 604–531 B.C., Chinese philosopher and
> founder of Taoism. From *Tao Te Ching*

Corporations today need to compete in the global marketplace. Because of this and other trends, many corporations are finding that old management styles just don't work anymore, so they are turning to new ways of managing people and projects. In this chapter, we'll take a look at some characteristics of good managers. We'll also examine how management styles are changing, especially in the multicultural workplace.

PART I

Preparation

LEARNING STRATEGY

Forming Concepts: Expressing ideas rapidly when you brainstorm improves your fluency.

A. BRAINSTORMING

With your business team, look at these pictures, discuss them, and write out your answers to the following questions:

- What does it take to be a good manager in today's corporation?
- Do men manage employees differently from women? If so, how?
- Do leadership qualities vary from culture to culture? In what ways?

B. WORKING WITH CONCEPTS: WHAT MAKES A GOOD MANAGER?

We asked three employees at large corporations the following question: "What characteristics or personal qualities make a good manager?" Read their responses:

1. Rafael Vasquez, analyst programmer, large clothing manufacturer:

   "A good manager has the same qualities as a good leader: somebody who's respected, who can be trusted. Good managers are people who can project their vision of the future. They recognize the achievements of others and can coach others so they develop and use their skills to the fullest. Good managers can also create an environment in which diverse opinions are valued, and everyone works together in order to find the best solutions to problems."

2. Linda Schuman, attorney, long-distance telecommunications company:

   "A good manager needs to be able to define and communicate to others the overall goals of the organization. He or she must also be able to determine what needs to be done in order to achieve the organization's goals. Finally, a good manager needs to know how to recognize and appeal to people's motives so they can be really productive."

3. Sam Yee, information resources manager, regional telephone company:

   "In my opinion, having good communication skills is essential. A good manager is able to communicate well both verbally and in writing. Having good judgment is also important. You have to be able to make decisions quickly and to hire good people. Good managers are open to change, especially in these times when things are changing so rapidly. Also, you can't *just* be a manager—you have to bring more to the table—for example, technical or financial skills—in addition to management skills. A good manager should also be fair, compassionate, and understanding."

With your business team, discuss the following questions about the responses you've just read, and write out your answers.

1. Why is it important for a manager to recognize the achievements of others and to be able to coach them, according to the programmer at the clothing manufacturer?
2. According to the attorney from the long-distance telephone company, why does a manager need to recognize and appeal to people's motives?
3. Why does a manager have to have good judgment, according to the manager from the regional phone company?

Remembering New Material: Understanding new words in context helps you remember their meanings.

C. JARGON, BUZZWORDS, AND SLANG: MANAGEMENT TALK

With your business team, suggest paraphrases for each of the following management buzzwords that the people in Exercise B used.

EXAMPLE "to project a vision" → To explain clearly to your co-workers or employees how you see the direction in which a project, a department, or the company as a whole should go.

Underline each one in its original context before you start.

to **project** a vision	to **recognize** achievements
to **coach** others	to **create** an environment
to **define** goals	to **communicate** goals
to **achieve** goals	to **appeal to** people's motives

D. PUTTING IT ALL TOGETHER

Your manager is going to retire soon. One of your associates will be promoted, taking the former manager's place. Your department head has asked your business team to write a memo describing the qualities and characteristics you would like to see in a manager.

Work with your business team. Take turns giving your ideas of what makes a good manager. Then, create a **consensus**—that is, try to agree as a group on a list of qualities. Create a statement that includes the main ideas of all group members and write it in the following memo form on a sheet of paper. You can use ideas from the responses in Exercise B, or create your own. When you write your statement, use the buzzwords or their paraphrases that you worked with in Exercise C.

[Your letterhead goes here.]

To: [Your department head's name goes here.]
From:
Date:
Re: Consensus on what makes a good manager

[The body of your memo goes here.]

E. DEBRIEFING MEETING

In a company meeting, compare your business team's statement on what makes a good manager with memos from other teams. What characteristics did every team agree on? What characteristics were important to only some of the teams?

F. SETTING OBJECTIVES

Following are the goals for this chapter. Read them, and consider your personal goals for the chapter. At the end of this chapter, on page 85, you'll list your results.

OBJECTIVES

Business
1. To define what a good manager is
2. To learn about different management styles
3. To learn about cultural differences in management styles
4. To understand the challenges facing managers in the multicultural workplace
5. To select a management style for a particular project, use it, and then assess its effectiveness

Language
6. To practice coming to a consensus (making a group decision)
7. To understand and be able to use words and expressions related to the topic of management
8. To recognize the use of the passive voice in business writing

Personal

_____

_____

_____

  **PART II**

Integration

A. TEAM MANAGEMENT

Many multinational organizations today are finding that a hierarchical (authoritarian) style of management, where managers control the details of what workers do, no longer works. They are replacing it with **team management.** Team management facilitates the personal power of workers. It allows employees to acknowledge and act on their own authority, and it encourages self-expression. Team management offers employees freedom, but they must be accountable for their actions.

Following is a selection from Philip R. Harris and Robert T. Moran's book, *Managing Cultural Differences: High-Performance Strategies for a New World of Business.* In it, the authors give some background on the causes and effects of team management (also called **matrix management**), and they offer some guidelines for evaluating the effectiveness of management teams. Moran and Harris think that team management is better for the global, multicultural workplace because it allows for **synergy,** or cooperative action.

Before you read the selection, write out the answers to these questions, and then discuss your answers with your business team:

1. Do you know of any corporations that currently have a hierarchical management style? Give an example of how you think it works.
2. Do you know of any corporations that use team management? Give an example of how you think it works.

As you read, look for answers to these questions:

1. What characteristics or qualities should a good team manager have?
2. What characteristics should an effective team have?

Managers as influencers of team cultures

by Philip R. Harris and Robert T. Moran

Changing technology and markets have stimulated the team approach to management. Inflation, resource scarcity, reduced personnel levels, budget cuts, and similar constraints have all underscored the need for better coordination and synergy in organizations. Team management provides for this coordination and synergy. Team management is found not only in industry, but also in insurance, banking, accounting, law, securities, retailing, construction, education, and health and human services.

Team management calls for new skills if personnel potential is to be fully realized. Although a team may be composed of knowledgeable people, they must learn new ways of relating and working together to solve cross-functional problems and to attain synergy. When teams consist of experienced employees from hierarchical organizations who have been conditioned to traditional organizational culture, synergy may not occur naturally—it may need to be created. Furthermore, the issue is not just how the team can function more synergistically, but how it integrates with the overall organization or society that it supposedly serves.

A group of individuals is not automatically a team; therefore, team building may be necessary in order to improve the group's performance. Casse (1982) suggests that the synergistic process within teams must be organized, promoted, and managed. He believes that team synergy results when members go beyond their individual capabilities—beyond what each is used to being and doing. Together the team may then produce something new, unique, and superior to that of any one member. For this to happen, he suggests that multicultural managers exhibit understanding of their own and others' cultural influences and limitations. They should also cultivate such skills as toleration of ambiguity, persistence, and patience, as well as assertiveness. If a team manager exemplifies such qualities, then the team as a whole will be better able to realize their potential and achieve their objectives.

An effective team can be characterized by the following six features:

1. Leadership—Is substantial confidence shown in team members? Are they free to discuss pertinent ideas, and is each one's contributions sought and used fully?
2. Motivation—Are the predominant motivators involvement, recognition, and rewards? Does each member feel equally responsible for mission achievement, and do all engage in cooperative effort?

3. Communications—Is the information flow within the team circular and shared equally? Is the upward and intergroup communication as authentic and accurate as it is within the team? How sensitive and aware are members of their colleagues' problems and concerns?

4. Decisions—Are members fully involved in decisions within the group, and is consensus sought when feasible?

5. Goals—Does the setting of team goals involve a group action, and is resistance confronted and channeled into agreement?

6. Control—Are team review and control functions shared? Are data gathered by the group used for self-guidance and problem solving? Are cliques undermining team energies?

Excerpted and adapted from Managing Cultural Differences: High-Performance Strategies for a New World of Business, 3rd ed., Philip R. Harris and Robert T. Moran. Gulf Publishing Company, 1991. Pp. 178, 179-180, 196.

B. ANALYZING WHAT YOU'VE READ

With your business team, write out your answers to the following questions about the passage you just read.

1. What are some of the factors that cause businesses to turn to team management?
2. List at least three types of businesses that are moving to team management.
3. Why may synergy not occur naturally when teams are composed of employees from hierarchical organizations?
4. What qualities should team managers have?
5. In the following chart, state in your own words one example for each feature of effective team behavior:

FEATURE	EXAMPLE
1. Leadership	*The team leader shows confidence in the members' abilities.*
2. Motivation	
3. Communication	
4. Decisions	
5. Goals	
6. Control	

Communication Memo • Communication Memo • Communication Memo

To: All Employees
From: Corporate Communications Department
Re: Use of the passive voice

Because business writers often use the passive voice, we suggest you review the following information regarding this form. The *Corporate Communications Policy Manual* suggests that you avoid using the passive voice in *your* writing because it is indirect; however, it is important to be able to recognize it when you read.

Review →   In a passive sentence, the object of the main verb in the sentence becomes the subject, and the verb is in the form of *be* + past participle.

subject	***be* + past participle**
EXAMPLE The team leader	was elected.

Note that:

- The verb *be* can be in any tense.
- The agent of the verb (the person or thing causing the action) is often not stated. In the example, the agent is understood (e.g., "by the team members").

In the active voice, you would write the sentence this way:

"The team members elected the team leader."

Please fill out the enclosed attachment and return it to your department head.

Enc.
CM/lb

Memo Attachment

Read the following sentences. Some are in the passive voice, and some are in the active voice. If the sentence is in the passive voice, put "P" next to it; if it's active, put "A" next to it. For every passive sentence, draw one line under the subject and two lines under the *be* form of the verb and the past participle. (Remember, the use of *be* + past participle usually means that the sentence is passive.)

EXAMPLE   *P*   A <u>team</u> may be <u>composed</u> of knowledgeable people.

_____ **1.** An effective team can be characterized by six features.

_____ **2.** Managers should also cultivate such skills as tolerance of ambiguity, persistence, and patience.

_____ **3.** In an effective team, substantial confidence is shown in the team members.

_____ **4.** A group of individuals is not automatically a team.

5. Team management is found not only in industry.

6. Teams often consist of experienced employees from hierarchical organizations who have been conditioned to traditional organizational culture.

7. In an effective team, team review and control functions are shared by all team members.

8. Additionally, consensus is sought whenever it is feasible.

C. JARGON, BUZZWORDS, AND SLANG: TEAM MANAGEMENT TALK

Working with an associate, draw lines to match the following team management buzzwords on the left (from the article, "Managers as Influencers of Team Cultures") with their definitions on the right. Underline the words in the article before you start.

BUZZWORDS
synergy
cross-functional
motivators
mission achievement
feasible
cliques

DEFINITIONS
smaller groups within bigger ones
getting the job done
cooperative action
possible
involving several skills at once
things that make people want
    to do a good job

D. PUTTING IT ALL TOGETHER

Working with a business team, practice your management skills by doing one of the following projects. Read the possibilities, and then reach a consensus about which project to do—that is, decide as a group. (Be realistic about the time and resources you have available.)

• Publish a company newsletter
• Organize a company picnic
• Arrange to have a guest speaker talk to your department
• Organize a company sports day
• Other ideas for projects (Write them down.)

Now, follow these steps:

1. Decide as a team how to manage the project—hierarchically or by team management. Select a project manager from your department (by tossing a coin, voting, or drawing names from a hat, for example). Then, according to the type of management you chose, decide what needs to be done and who will perform the tasks.
2. Implement the project—that is, do it!
3. When you are finished, evaluate your project and your project manager. Use the questions that appear in the article, "Managers as Influencers of Team Cultures," on pages 74-75.

4. Write your evaluation in a memo to your CEO. Before you send it to the CEO, get together with another business team and compare evaluations. As you write, keep in mind the corporate policy regarding the use of the passive voice, and try to use some buzzwords you picked up from the reading on team management, or the responses in Part I, Exercise B, page 71. You can use the following memo form:

[Your letterhead goes here.]

To:
From:
Date:
Re: Evaluation of [project name]

[Write the body of your memo here.]

E. MANAGING DIVERSITY

Following is an excerpt of an article on managing diversity from *Working Woman* magazine. Managing diversity means understanding and valuing differences among people in the workplace. Differences might include culture, gender, sexual orientation, physical disabilities, or learning and working styles.

Before you read, discuss your answers to these questions with your business team:

1. What is unique about you that you might bring to a work situation? Consider such things as:
   • your gender
   • your country or culture of origin
   • your learning or work style
   • any disabilities you might have
   • anything else that makes you special
2. If you were a manager, how might these qualities influence your management style?

As you read, look for answers to these questions:

1. Does the author of this article think that people from different cultures have different management styles?
2. Many articles on diversity in the workplace *simplify* cultural and gender differences among people. Sometimes this leads to stereotyping. In your opinion, is this author oversimplifying cultural and gender characteristics?

The enlightened manager: how to treat all your employees fairly

by Audrey Edwards

The American workplace is changing—in gender, color, nationality, and cultural points of view. By the year 2000, according to the Bureau of Labor Statistics, white males will account for only 32 percent of the entering work force. The implications are profound. The ability of American business to recover lost productivity, regain its competitive edge and move into the 21st century with a renewed sense of preeminence will depend precisely on its ability to effectively attract and manage the diverse talent that will characterize its new work force.

Managing diversity means opportunity. The labor market is going to look and be different. The challenge, then, is in learning how to manage this difference. And the manager who can successfully do so will be as indispensable to corporate management as working capital.

In response to this challenge, management consultant Iris Randall trains managers to become aware of and to value diversity. She has managers fill out a personal-profile questionnaire used by human-resource trainers to help employees assess their behavioral styles. The Personal Profile System, developed by Performax Systems International, identifies four styles of behavior. Randall explains the four styles and the differences among them, then tells managers which category they fit into.

The first style is the D, or dominant, behavior. "People with high D, Donald Trump-type dominant behavior," says Randall, "make decisions rapidly. They're interested in results, the bottom line." Of course, individuals from all cultural backgrounds fall into this category, but Randall says most often it's people with a Euro-American background, particularly white males, who exhibit it.

The second style is I, for influencers. "African-Americans, Hispanics and women in general exhibit more I behavior," contends Randall. "These types are very verbal. They are good at influencing and persuading. They are the cheerleaders: 'I can, you can, we can make a difference.' They like people, and they like applause."

C is the cautious style, more frequently seen among Asians, believes Randall. "They are taught not to shoot from the hip, not to be confrontational, always to think before they speak, to make sure they are right." And S, or steady, behavior is, Randall feels, more often found among Native Americans. "For the most part, they show the high S behavior of a person who will hang in there. They are good team players and have no trouble recognizing the person in charge, whereas D-behavior types all act as if they are the boss."

Of course, to assume that all people from these respective cultures will exhibit these behaviors is to perpetuate more stereotypes. Focusing on culture and behavior—your own as well as those of people different from you—simply helps you develop insight into different mindsets, which is crucial for managing cultural diversity. "If you're a manager and you're looking for higher productivity out of your people, and if you realize that you can get it by understanding how they tend to behave and by talking their language, hopefully you will learn to do it," says Randall. Once you do, the payoff will be increased productivity and decreased conflict.

Adapted from "The Enlightened Manager: How To Treat All Employees Fairly," by Audrey Edwards, January 1991.

F. ANALYZING WHAT YOU'VE READ

Check your comprehension of the article you just read by completing the following activities:

LEARNING STRATEGY

Forming Concepts: Organizing your ideas in a chart or a list helps you to see the relationships between management styles, personality types, and culture.

1. Complete the following chart. Describe the characteristics that are associated with each of the management styles outlined in the article. Then give examples of people or cultures that fit into each category, according to Randall. Note the examples.

MANAGEMENT STYLE	D DOMINANT	I INFLUENCERS	C CAUTIOUS	S STEADY
Characteristics	_____ _____ _____ _____	*verbal* _____ _____ _____	_____ _____ _____ _____	_____ _____ _____ _____
People, Cultures	_____ _____ _____ _____	*women* _____ _____ _____	_____ _____ _____ _____	_____ _____ _____ _____

2. Randall has associated particular cultural groups and genders with four management styles. Do you agree with her classifications? For example, do you agree that women generally are I-types, that Asians tend to be C-types, and so on? Can you think of any exceptions? What are they?

3. Which style describes you? Does your culture match Randall's definitions? Why or why not? Does your gender match? Why or why not?

G. JARGON, BUZZWORDS, AND SLANG: BUSINESS SLANG

The author of "The Enlightened Manager" uses the following informal and idiomatic expressions in her article. Find the words and expressions in their contexts in the article and underline them. Then match the idiomatic expression on the right with its synonym on the left.

EXPRESSION	SYNONYM
bottom line	reward
cheerleaders	to make a quick decision
to shoot from the hip	the financial outcomes
will hang in there	of a business venture
mindsets	ways of thinking
payoff	enthusiastic people
	will be persistent

LEARNING STRATEGY

Remembering New Material: Using words you've just learned helps you remember their meanings.

Now, work with an associate and take turns restating in your own words each sentence from the article containing the idioms. You can use the synonyms here or think of others.

H. PUTTING IT ALL TOGETHER

With a business team, discuss possible problems that could arise between people having these different management styles and write out your conclusions.

- You are a female D-style manager, and you have a male C-style employee.
- You are a female I-style manager, and you have a male D-style employee.
- You are a male S-style manager and you have several male D-style employees.

Now, choose one of the preceding combinations of styles. Using the management styles described in the article, role-play the following with an associate. One plays the role of the manager, the other is the employee:

- The manager suggests that the employee take a diversity training course that the company is offering. The employee asks the manager for the reasons behind his or her suggestion.

Perform the role-play for the other members of your business team. Then evaluate how the manager and the employee communicated using the following chart. Check whether you thought your associates' form, tone, and nonverbal behavior were appropriate or inappropriate. Then give comments and suggestions to your associates for each feature.

Associate A (manager)

FEATURE	APPROPRIATE	INAPPROPRIATE	COMMENTS AND SUGGESTIONS
Form			
Tone			
Nonverbal behavior			

Associate B (employee)

FEATURE	APPROPRIATE	INAPPROPRIATE	COMMENTS AND SUGGESTIONS
Form			
Tone			
Nonverbal behavior			

I. LISTENING: INTERVIEW WITH AN INFORMATION RESOURCES MANAGER

You are going to hear an interview with Craig Lee, an information resources manager at an international garment manufacturing and marketing company. Before you listen, take a look at the following buzzwords:

- **admin**
- **to bring something to the table**
- **to put in eight hours**

EXAMPLE "More and more, managers are really **bringing to the table** some expertise, whether it be in data processing or in finance, as well as taking care of some of the **admin stuff**. . . . At my previous company, I was there to make sure people **put in their eight hours.**"

In a business team, state what you think these terms mean. Think of another way to say them and share your ideas with your team members.

LEARNING STRATEGY

Managing Your Learning: Having an expectation of what you are going to hear can improve your comprehension.

Now, listen to the interview once and answer these questions:

1. How many people report to Craig? Write the number here: _____

2. Has Craig's management style changed since he's been at his present company? Circle your answer.
   YES   NO

[Now, listen to the speaker.]

Listen to Craig's interview once or twice again, and answer the following questions:

1. Why is his group so small?
2. Craig uses this expression: "the care and feeding of the staff." He gives a synonym for the expression in the same sentence. What is another way of saying "the care and feeding of the staff"?
3. What is the role of the manager where Craig works now?
4. List two adjectives that Craig uses to describe his management style.
5. List three examples for each of the two management styles Craig compares, his old style and his new style.

OLD STYLE: COMMAND-AND-CONTROL	NEW STYLE: EMPOWERMENT
Example 1 *Not trusting*	Example 1
Example 2	Example 2
Example 3	Example 3

[Listen again]

J. PUTTING IT ALL TOGETHER

Interview someone who works or has worked in business—a friend, a family member, or a classmate. Ask him or her about the management style at the company he or she works (or worked) for. Take notes on your interview, and share your results with your business team. You can ask the following questions, or think of your own.

NOTE Put the questions into the past tense if the interviewee is no longer working.

Name: _____

Company Name: _____

1. What is the predominant management style at your company?
2. Is this style typical of most companies you are familiar with?
3. (If your interviewee is a manager:)
   a. How would you describe your management style?
   b. Has your management style changed since you've been at your company? If so, how?
4. (If your interviewee is not a manager:)
   a. How would you describe your manager's style?
   b. Has his or her management style changed since you've been at your company? If so, how?
5. Ask additional questions of your own.

When you are finished, report on your interview to your business team.

Evaluation

Managing Your Learning: Keeping track of what you have learned and what you still want to work on helps you become an independent learner.

How well did you achieve the objectives for this chapter? List your results. Use the prompts that accompany each objective.

OBJECTIVES	RESULTS
Business 1. To define what a good manager is 2. To learn about different management styles 3. To learn about cultural differences in management styles 4. To understand the challenges facing managers in the multicultural workplace 5. To select a management style for a particular project, use it, and then assess its effectiveness	**Business** 1. Write your definition of what a good manager is. 2. Give examples of two management styles. 3. Give examples of at least two cultural differences in management styles. 4. Describe one challenge a manager in a multicultural work environment might face. 5. Summarize in one sentence your evaluation of the project you did in Part II, Exercise D, page 77.
Language 6. To practice coming to a consensus (making a group decision) 7. To understand and be able to use words and expressions related to the topic of management 8. To understand the use of the passive voice in business writing	**Language** 6. Describe in a few sentences the process of coming to a consensus (see Part I, Exercise D, page 72). 7. Write three new buzzwords or expressions you learned in this chapter. 8. Find one passive sentence from one of the articles you read in this chapter and write it down.
Personal _____ _____ _____	**Personal** _____ _____ _____

Now answer the following questions:

• What are your strengths in the area of management?
• How can you continue to learn about management on your own?

Marketing: Products and Services for Today's Consumer

CHAPTER PREVIEW

In this chapter you'll

- learn about the "4 Ps" of marketing.
- examine how marketing strategies have changed to meet the needs of today's consumers.
- explore and develop promotional strategies.
- predict future consumer needs and create marketing strategies to meet them.
- improve your English skills by conducting out-of-class interviews.

If it's one thing about our business that people don't understand enough, it's that our strategy puts us extremely close to our customer, which is in stark contrast to the traditional approach of corporations designing what they think is right and hoping consumers will buy it.

—Michael Dell, Dell Computers CEO

How have advanced telecommunications systems made it easier for companies to reach their consumers? How have companies had to adapt traditional marketing strategies to meet the needs of today's sophisticated consumer more efficiently? In this chapter, you will form your own answers to these questions by examining how innovative companies are restructuring their methods in the following areas, known as the "4 Ps" of marketing: (1) product, (2) place (distribution), (3) promotion, and (4) pricing.

PART I

Preparation

A. BRAINSTORMING

With your business team, look at the photos, discuss them, and write your answers to the questions that follow.

1. What do these products do for the consumers using them?
2. What do you think these consumers do when they have questions or problems regarding these products?
3. How do companies know what consumers want?

B. WORKING WITH CONCEPTS: PRODUCTS AND SERVICES

The following article explains how successful companies in the '90s are offering consumers more than just products: the opportunity to establish long-term, mutually beneficial relationships. Before you read, discuss the following with an associate, and write out your responses.

1. Many companies are finding ways to keep in contact with their customers after they have bought a particular product. List some advantages of doing this for both the company and the consumer.
2. Give two examples of how companies can "share" customers. For example, if you fly a certain airline, you'll get a discount at a specified hotel.

There are no products—only services

by Thomas A. Stewart

Take a step beyond "total quality" and "customer satisfaction." There's a new view of the relationship between supplier and customer, and even which is which. The idea, as put by Rosabeth Moss Katner of the Harvard Business School: Think of every product you buy or sell as a service. In other words, look at what it does, not what it is.

That way, selling a product becomes only one of your opportunities to do something for your customer. Many companies are now offering additional services, particularly post-sale services, to increase the value of their products. This practice, often referred to as "bundling," is an effective way to keep in contact with customers. Look at Toyota's Lexus. Thanks to a partnership with IBM, Lexus tracks every car on a national computer—your sedan's complete maintenance history is available to every dealer from Miami to Seattle. Why? Because Lexus doesn't want its relationship with you to end at the showroom door.

At Packaging Corp. of America, employees say they offer packaging *solutions,* not just packaging. Says CEO, Monte Hayman: "It used to be that we made a product and looked for people to buy it. Then we started doing research to learn what the market wanted, and developed product for that.

Today we're working with individual customers." That means turning the company's manufacturing divisions—which specialize in materials like corrugated cardboard and plastic—into service arms that often work together to provide what customers want.

Then there's *unbundling.* When you want to offer more products and services, but it isn't within your means to produce them yourself, you might decide to contract out stuff that you would never have let out of your sight before. IBM no longer handles its own warehousing. Two years ago it junked 21 parts warehouses in favor of half-a-dozen outside vendors.

Commodore Business Machines goes further: In November it unbundled virtually all of its post-sale services for consumer products. Its partner is a new division of Federal Express called Business Logistics Services. Fed Ex mans a 24-hour help line for Commodore. If your computer needs to go to the shop, Fed Ex will pick it up the morning after you call, drop off a replacement, and often do the repairs at its Memphis hub. Customers never know they're dealing with Fed Ex employees, except for the delivery man. After a six-month trial, says Jim Reeder, Commodore's vice president for customer satisfaction, his company is offering better service at half the previous cost.

This kind of collaboration is replacing competition in relationships with suppliers. Experts at the Cresap

consulting firm call it "supplier integration." It elevates outsourcing from a mere cost-cutting measure to the level of strategy. The new goal is a win-win alliance, where suppliers get the security of a long-term relationship and customers get more say over their upstream processes.

In an integrated relationship, instead of pitting suppliers against one another to get the best price, purchasing agents work closely with a few select suppliers to reduce the total cost of the deal. Often, as in the arrangement between Fed Ex and Commodore, it is difficult to find the line between supplier and customer.

Companies that think of the products they buy and sell as services can also discover new ways to market existing products, as Xerox did when it redefined its copier machine business as *document processing.* At General Electric, the *workout program,* a continuing series of "town meetings" where employees look for ways to improve processes, has expanded to include joint sessions with customers like Sears. They study such questions as whether to share a single system to track purchase orders. The new slogan: "GE and its customers—one system, not two systems."

Excerpted and adapted from "There Are No Products—Only Services," by Thomas A. Stewart. Fortune magazine, January 14, 1991.

C. JARGON, BUZZWORDS, AND SLANG: PRODUCTS AS SERVICES

Read these expressions from the passage. In the exercise that follows, you are given part of the meaning of each expression. Use the partial meaning to guess which of the definitions is correct. Circle your choice.

supplier integration   service arms
bundling   post-sale services
contracting out   unbundling

LEARNING STRATEGY

Managing Your Learning: You can figure out the meaning of an unfamiliar expression by analyzing the part of the expression you already know.

EXAMPLE   outsourcing:
A *source* is where something comes from, so when companies "outsource," it probably means they

a. buy or hire additional products/services from other companies.
b. create additional products/services inside the company.
c. share their customers with other companies.

1. supplier integration
   To *integrate* means to blend or combine, so supplier integration probably means
   a. a supplier sells directly to the consumer.
   b. suppliers work together to offer consumers more services.
   c. a supplier offers several different services.

2. bundling
   To *bundle* means to put several items together in one package, so "bundling" is when companies
   a. offer one service for one price.
   b. offer many services separately.
   c. offer several services as one "package."

3. contracting out
   A *contract* is a formal agreement for certain services at an agreed-upon price, so when a company "contracts out" it probably
   a. hires other companies to perform some of its services.
   b. performs services for other companies.
   c. has no current agreements with other companies.

4. <u>service arms</u>

  Arms extend from a larger body, so "service arms" of a company are probably

 a. long hallways attached to a large office.

 b. services that keep track of customer needs for a long time.

 c. departments within a company that deal with specific customer services.

5. <u>post-sale services</u>

  Post means *after,* so "post-sale services" are probably

 a. services offered to customers before they buy a product on sale.

 b. services offered to customers after they buy a product.

 c. sale prices offered to customers after the sale is over.

6. <u>unbundling</u>

  To *unbundle* is to separate items that were once together, so when a company "unbundles" services, it probably

 a. decreases services in its service package.

 b. increases services in its service package.

 c. hires other companies to supply the separate services offered in its service package.

Communication Memo • Communication Memo • Communication Memo

> To: All Employees
> From: Corporate Communications Department
> Re: *By*-phrases to describe a plan and its effect

By-phrases will help you explain clearly how a marketing plan is implemented and what effects the plan will have.

EXAMPLE <u>By working together</u>, companies are finding ways to "share" their customers.

Note the following in this structure:

- The *by*-phrase introduces the cause, or action, that takes place.
- The accompanying phrase expresses the effects of the action indicated in the *by*-phrase.
- A *by*-phrase can be used at the beginning, as in the previous example. It can also be used at the end or even in the middle of a sentence, as illustrated in the following examples:

EXAMPLES Companies "share" their customers <u>by working together</u>.
      Companies, <u>by working together</u>, "share" their customers.

- When the *by*-phrase is at the end of the sentence, there is no need for a comma.

Enc.
CM/ja

Memo Attachment

Using the phrases and information from the reading, complete the following sentences.

EXAMPLES Phrase—<u>Companies / offering service packages</u>
Sentence—<u>By offering service packages,</u> companies are able to increase the value of their products.
Phrase—<u>IBM / warehousing its own inventory</u>
Sentence—<u>IBM</u> saves a tremendous amount of money <u>by not warehousing its own inventory</u>.

1. <u>Lexus/tracking every car on a computer</u>
2. <u>Packaging Corp./turning manufacturing divisions into service arms</u>
3. <u>Commodore/unbundling all its post sale services</u>
4. <u>suppliers/integrating their services</u>
5. <u>GE/holding a series of town meetings</u>

D. PUTTING IT ALL TOGETHER

Scan the article, "There Are No Products—Only Services," for the paragraph about Commodore Business Machines. Review the partnership between Commodore and Federal Express. In a business team, briefly discuss how both companies and their customers benefit from this arrangement. Then do the following activity together.

1. Your team is a marketing department in a company of your choice. You want to create a "supplier integration" agreement with another company to better serve the needs of your customers. The following list of companies will help you brainstorm for ideas about a mutually beneficial partnership between two companies. For example, when you purchase items at the campus bookstore, you get a coupon for computer rentals.

furniture store	campus bookstore
auto company	golf courses
computer rentals	alterations
interior decorator	cellular phones
car rentals	TV/stereo store
battery manufacturer	credit card company
dry cleaners	housekeeping service

2. Complete the "Marketing Partnership Proposal" on page 93 with your team.

MARKETING PARTNERSHIP PROPOSAL

Companies for proposed partnership:

1. _____

2. _____

Product/Service description (what each company will provide):

_____
_____
_____
_____

Benefits to Company #1:

_____
_____
_____

Benefits to Company #2:

_____
_____
_____

Benefits to customers:

_____
_____
_____

How will long-term relationship with customer be maintained?

_____
_____
_____

How might customers' needs change in the future?

_____
_____

How would you change your service package to meet these new needs?

_____
_____

Threads

Don't forget that your product or service is not differentiated until the customer understands the difference.

Tom Peters, Business Writer

E. DEBRIEFING MEETING

Meet with another business team and share your partnership proposals. Discuss each plan's strengths and weaknesses, and offer suggestions for improvement.

F. SETTING OBJECTIVES

Following are the goals for this chapter. Read them, and consider your personal goals for the chapter. At the end of this chapter, on page 107, you'll list your results.

OBJECTIVES

Business

1. To learn about the "4 Ps" of marketing
2. To discover how new marketing strategies reflect the current needs of today's consumer
3. To predict consumer needs and create a marketing plan that meets them
4. To evaluate various promotional strategies and determine how efficient they will be in reaching target markets
5. To develop your own plans for successfully marketing a product

Language

6. To understand and be able to use words and expressions related to the topic of marketing
7. To describe how marketing plans work using *by*-phrases
8. To improve your English conversation skills by conducting out-of-class interviews

Personal

_____

_____

_____

_____

_____

_____

Integration

A. JUST-IN-TIME RETAILING: ELIMINATING THE MIDDLEMAN

You are going to read an article about how companies are changing their distribution methods to give today's customers what they want: a less expensive, more convenient way to get products and services. Before you read the article, discuss the following questions with an associate and write out the answers. The questions will help you predict some of the marketing concepts explored in the article.

LEARNING STRATEGY

Forming Concepts: Discussing a topic before you read about it helps you find out what you already know and what you need to learn.

1. Traditionally, manufacturers have sold their products to stores through a "middleman." What do you think the role of the middleman is?
2. A recent study conducted by Stillerman-Jones & Co., an Indianapolis-based consulting firm, cited that in 1992 the average consumer shopped for 72 minutes at 2.6 stores every time they went to the mall, a decrease of 18 minutes spent and one less store visited by the average consumer in 1982. What are some reasons people may be spending less time in stores? How do consumers get products if they don't go out and buy them?
3. The following article is titled, "The Fall of the Mall." What do you think it's going to be about?

The fall of the mall

by Gretchen Morgenson

Just-in-time retailing. In essence, it means making retailing more efficient by reducing the length of time, the quantity of inventory, and the number of middlemen that stand between a product and a consumer.

At the forefront of just-in-time retailing was, of course, Sam Walton. His huge investment in computer systems enabled him to get rid of many of the middlemen who clutter the path of merchandise and add to its cost as it moves from the factory to the consumer. With the computers, Wal-Mart can speed information on what's selling and what isn't from the marketplace directly to its suppliers; the manufacturers in turn use the information to produce what consumers want. Expenses for labor and working capital are cut, so the markup is minimal. The winners are Wal-Mart's consumers, its suppliers and its shareholders. The big losers are the traditional mom-and-pop merchants who can't compete with Wal-Mart, and the factories, wholesalers, regional reps, and other salespeople whose livelihoods depend on the mom-and-pops.

Stores have always thrived because they were the only places consumers could go to comparison shop. Retailers and salespeople wanted to keep it that way and put up barriers to prevent information from flowing freely. The ad would tempt you with a bargain-priced VCR; the salesman would push a different model, on which the store's markup was much fatter. You'd leave the store confused by all the model numbers and feature specifications.

The barriers to good information are crashing down. Thanks to the rapid increase of buying services, catalogs, and consumer product guides, shoppers no longer leave home to gather information. It's available by mail, phone, computer, or on television.

Don't consumers like to see, touch, and smell the goods they're thinking of buying? Of course they do, which is why stores will never disappear entirely. But note this: The store is fast becoming a place where people kick the tires, lift the lid on a washing machine, or listen to the sound of a stereo speaker—and then go home and call an (800) number to order the same item at a discount of 40 percent.

One of the oldest sayings about consumption in America goes like this: Washing machines, or cars, or stocks aren't bought; they're sold. Therefore, salesmen are needed.

If this line were ever accurate, it is becoming less so. Meet Walter Forbes. Ten years ago he cofounded CUC International, now one of the largest just-in-time retailers around. It offers consumers discounted prices, by computer or phone, on 250,000 brand-name products, including appliances, luggage, jewelry, telephones, cameras, and sporting equipment. A recent catalog, for example, offered a Toshiba color television for $399. Circuit City Stores sell the same TV for $599. Another buy: a Pierre Cardin five-piece luggage set for $129. List price, $630.

Here's how CUC works:

The cost to sign up with the company is $49 a year for phone members, $39 for on-line computer users. Suppose you want a Whirlpool washer. You place your order for the machine with CUC, which passes the order on to Whirlpool, which then ships the washer to you.

Think of all the costs CUC is eliminating—no store, no parking lot, no salesmen, no inventory, and considerably less insurance.

In the example above of buying a washing machine from CUC, the manufacturer, Whirlpool, delivered the product to the customer. This practice is called drop-shipping and it can eliminate a number of distribution costs, inventories, and warehousing costs among them. In effect, drop-shipped goods are warehoused at the manufacturer or, ideally, in the Federal Express or UPS system as the product travels from the factory to consumer.

On-line services requiring a PC, a modem, and a computer-literate consumer are few but growing. According to the Information & Interactive Services Report newsletter, subscribers to on-line services now number 3.5 million.

Color catalogs are already beaming down telephone lines. Twenty of the 100 merchants that sell goods on Compuserve do it with pictures. Land's End is one of them. The company's president, William End, admits that the graphics are still pretty crude, but he's convinced electronic shopping is going to be a big factor in retailing in the years ahead.

"We have five tests going now, including Prodigy, Compuserve, and GEnie," says End. "We're doing a reasonable amount of business to continue testing. My gut tells me there will be a fairly significant shift to this kind of business."

By the time the shift to just-in-time retailing is so identifiable that the newspapers write about it, the winners and losers will already be well established. Who will they be?

Among the winners, of course, will be the retailers and manufacturers that are already established within consumers' homes and continually improve their product offerings or their services. To satisfy consumers who still want to kick tires on a product before they buy it, manufacturers will likely set up showrooms in various cities or regions where consumers can go to inspect the merchandise.

According to Mark Walsh, the president of Information Kinetics, an on-line job placement agency, the just-in-time retailing trend is irreversible. Until a few months ago, Walsh was a vice president of CUC International and was one of the creators of that company's successful on-line shopping service. Says Walsh of the relationship between merchants and their customers: "There's a lot of hidden demand for what retailing doesn't do for us anymore, like offering convenience, fast service, and good prices. Today it's a dysfunctional system. As soon as consumers realize there are alternatives, there will be no effective argument that a retailer can make to convince smart shoppers to keep buying the same old way."

Excerpted and adapted from "The Fall of the Mall." Forbes magazine, May 24, 1993. Pgs. 106–112

B. ANALYZING WHAT YOU'VE READ

With your business team, complete the activities, and write out the answers to the following questions about the article you just read.

1. Explain the information illustrated in the following graphs from the article.
2. What does the information in the graphs tell you about the lifestyles and needs of today's consumers?
3. Does just-in-time retailing offer effective methods to meet today's consumers' needs?
4. The article states that, "By the time the shift to just-in-time retailing is so identifiable that the newspapers write about it, the winners and losers will already be well established." Following is a list of jobs. Decide which will be "winners"—profiting financially from just-in-time retailing—and which will be "losers"—suffering financially from just-in-time retailing. On a sheet of paper, identify each one as a "winner" or a "loser," and briefly explain your answers.
   a. UPS and FedEx drivers. Why?
   b. Cable TV network owners. Why?
   c. Shopping mall developers. Why?
   d. Magazine publishers. Why?
   e. Salespeople. Why?
5. List two more jobs or industries that you think will profit from just-in-time retailing.
6. The article suggests that the just-in-time retailing trend is "irreversible." In your opinion, what will happen to traditional retailing?

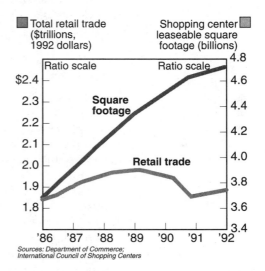

Sources: Department of Commerce; International Council of Shopping Centers

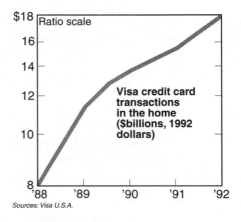

Sources: Visa U.S.A.

C. JARGON, BUZZWORDS, AND SLANG: RETAIL TALK

Read the following words and phrases from the article. Then, with an associate, carefully read the sentences and discuss the meaning of each underlined word or phrase. After deciding on the meaning of the word or phrase in each sentence, write out your own definition.

middleman	mom-and-pop	markup
drop-ship	buying services	kick the tires

1. With its computers, Wal-Mart can order or discontinue product directly from its suppliers. There's no need for a <u>middleman</u>.
2. Instead of warehousing products themselves, many catalog companies pass their customer orders on to a manufacturer. The manufacturer then <u>drop-ships</u> the merchandise directly to the customer.
3. Companies like Wal-Mart buy large quantities of merchandise at low prices and pass on the discount to consumers. Without the middleman, there's no need for a high <u>markup</u> on their original cost.
4. <u>Mom-and-pops</u> can't compete with the low prices that are offered in a just-in-time retailing system because they are too small to buy in large quantities.
5. More Americans are shopping by computer, television, or telephone. These <u>buying services</u> pose a serious challenge to the country's traditional retail industry.
6. In order to satisfy consumers who still want to <u>kick the tires</u> on a product before they buy it, manufacturers and just-in-time retailers will set up showrooms where consumers can go to inspect the merchandise.

D. PUTTING IT ALL TOGETHER

Your business team has been hired by a large just-in-time retailer similar to CUC International. Your assignment is to design a showroom where customers can come and "kick the tires" before they decide to buy. Begin by writing down your Showroom Proposal, using the following guidelines. Before writing, brainstorm with your team for a creative and effective design.

Showroom Proposal

1. **Product:** Make a list of the merchandise that will be displayed in the showroom—for example, automobiles, computers, furniture, clothing, and so on. Try to think of items that customers would like to inspect before buying.
2. **Distribution:** Describe the procedure that consumers and employees will follow to order the merchandise displayed in the showroom. Try to think of a system that will allow for the most orders in the shortest amount of time by using, for example, computers, interactive screens, or phones. Also, explain how the merchandise will get to the customers after they have ordered it at the showroom.
3. **Design:** Draw a diagram of the showroom floor. Label everything in the showroom as though you were making a detailed map. Label all entrances, product displays, ordering center, TV screens, etc.
4. **Personnel:** Approximately how many employees will you need to run the showroom? Explain what skills they will need and how they will use them.

Take a moment to observe a business team working on their showroom design. Are all team members contributing? Is everyone's opinion respected? Check whether you think the participants' level of formality, tone of voice, and nonverbal behavior are appropriate or inappropriate. Also write brief comments or suggestions.

FEATURE	APPROPRIATE	INAPPROPRIATE	COMMENTS AND SUGGESTIONS
Level of Formality			
Tone			
Nonverbal behavior			

E. PROMOTION: TARGETING YOUR MARKET

The article you are going to read is about two different promotional strategies for the same product. Keep the following questions in mind as you read.

1. What research did the companies mentioned in the article do before they promoted their products?
2. How effectively did each company apply their research data to their promotional strategies?

Advantage, Mitsubishi

by John Harris

The Plymouth Laser and the Mitsubishi Eclipse are identical sports coupes built by Diamondstar Motors, a 50-50 partnership between Chrysler and Mitsubishi. Last year Chrysler's 3,000 dealers sold 40,000 *Lasers* while Mitsubishi's *500* dealers sold 50,000 *Eclipses*! Here's a case where the products were more than just similar; they were identical. Yet, the Eclipse far outsold the Laser. Why?

Tiny Mitsubishi, just 1.5 percent of the U.S. auto market, compared with 10 percent for Chrysler's divisions, *outmaneuvered* Chrysler on the marketing front. Both Mitsubishi and Chrysler correctly identified the target market: educated professionals age 25–35 with incomes of $40,000 and up. They both figured that women would make up a bigger chunk of those buyers than men—Chrysler expected its buyers to be 65 percent female. But Chrysler and Mitsubishi went after their target market in very different ways.

Take the name. Mitsubishi, at the time still relatively unknown in the United States, correctly guessed that youthful customers are usually more willing to experiment with an unfamiliar name if they like how the car looks and performs. The name *Eclipse* suggested "a happening, a major event," says Mike Nash, Mitsubishi's vice president of marketing. Adds Richard Recchia, executive vice president for Mitsubishi, "We had to make this car come across as a very vibrant, young type of vehicle."

First, Mitsubishi started early and spent big. Several months before the vehicle's launch, it blitzed the market with a $35 million ad campaign for the Eclipse—37 percent of Mitsubishi's total 1989 advertising budget. Then Mitsubishi departed from traditional automotive marketing formulas by featuring women in its TV commercials and not focusing on the car's engineering specifications. Instead, Mitsubishi fashioned an image that an Eclipse was the "in" car to own.

Mitsubishi also noticed something else. "The people we wanted to get in the car were working out in a gym every day," says Nash. Mitsubishi sponsored a contest among aerobics instructors, awarding cars to the two who signed up the most class members for test drives. Result: 5,000 test drives! Mitsubishi tried other stunts too, including a key-in-the-bottle promotion with *Agree* shampoo.

Chrysler? With a total of 17 car models to sell, it had fewer dollars to put toward the Laser than Mitsubishi did for the Eclipse—Mitsubishi had only five models. But Chrysler was less daring in their promotion strategies, sticking with a more traditional ad campaign. Most Laser ads showed up in car magazines, which reach relatively few women, and the Laser's *only* TV spot focused on the car's horsepower and speed. Chrysler's *Plymouth* label also worked against reaching their target market—the typical Plymouth buyer is 40-plus years old.

Excerpted and adapted from "Advantage, Mitsubishi," by John Harris. Forbes, March 18, 1991. Pgs. 100, 104.

Threads

From 1973–83 Procter & Gamble lost more than $250 million in Japan. Why? American diapers didn't fit Japanese babies and soap advertisements were culturally inappropriate.

Stephen J. Simurda, *Business Entrepreneur, 5/94*

F. ANALYZING WHAT YOU'VE READ

Check your understanding of the information in "Advantage, Mitsubishi" by completing the following activities with a business team.

1. The following chart contains the information from the article about the *target market*, correctly identified by both Mitsubishi and Chrysler. Use your imagination to come up with examples of probable professions and hobbies for this group of people.

TARGET MARKET—ECLIPSE & LASER

Age	25–35
Gender	Over 60% female
Income	$40,000 and up
Education	College graduates
Professions	_____
	_____
	_____
	_____
	_____
	_____
Hobbies	_____
	_____
	_____
	_____
	_____

2. Complete the chart with notes about the different strategies used by Mitsubishi and Chrysler to promote the Eclipse and the Laser. Scan the article and use your imagination for the information you will need.

PROMOTION STRATEGIES

	MITSUBISHI	CHRYSLER
Magazine Advertisements	_____	*car magazines*
	_____	_____
TV Commercials	_____	_____
	_____	_____
Special Promotions	_____	_____
	_____	_____

3. Think about the joint promotion that Mitsubishi did with Agree shampoo. How do you think it worked?

4. List four joint promotional ad campaigns that you've heard about.

G. JARGON, BUZZWORDS, AND SLANG: PROMOTIONAL TALK

Read the following verb phrases from the article. Each verb phrase appears in a partial sentence. With an associate, scan the article for information, and, on a sheet of paper, complete the sentences and write a definition for each verb phrase.

to outmaneuver a competitor   to blitz the market
to fashion an image   to reach a target market

1. Mitsubishi fashioned an image for the Eclipse that made the car seem . . .
   To fashion an image is to . . .
2. One of the reasons Chrysler did not reach their target market is because . . .
   To reach a target market is to . . .
3. Mitsubishi blitzed the market by getting its ads out in many forms such as . . .
   To blitz the market is to . . .
4. Tiny Mitsubishi outmaneuvered Chrysler . . .
   To outmaneuver is to . . .

H. PUTTING IT ALL TOGETHER

Work with an associate to create your own promotion campaign for a product or service, either real or imaginary. Use the promotion preparation sheet on page 103 to organize your ideas about your product, your target market, and your promotion campaign.

LEARNING STRATEGY

Overcoming Limitations: You can increase your understanding of a new topic by incorporating what you've learned in a related project.

PROMOTION PREPARATION SHEET

Product Name	**Product Description**

Target Market

Age: _____   Income: _____

Gender: _____   Education: _____

Professions: _____

_____

_____

Hobbies: _____

_____

_____

Campaign

Modes of advertising (e.g., magazines, billboards):

_____

_____

_____

Focus of advertisements:

_____

_____

_____

_____

_____

_____

Joint promotion idea:

_____

_____

_____

_____

_____

_____

I. PRICING: LISTENING TO THE CUSTOMER

Listen to what Michael Modello, vice president of marketing at Celestial Seasonings in Boulder, Colorado, has to say about the way customers view pricing. Before you listen, discuss and answer the following questions in a business team.

1. How do you decide if the product or service you're thinking of buying is worth the price?
2. If you were ready to begin marketing a new product, how would you find out what customers would be willing to pay for it?

Before you listen to the speaker's views on pricing, read the following statements. Then listen, and for each of the statements mark either "T" (true), "F" (false), or "?" (not enough information).

	T	F	?
1. The way to find out what customers will pay is to ask them on the phone.	——	——	——
2. Customer input is often predictable.	——	——	——
3. It is best to price below what customers expect to pay.	——	——	——
4. Too low a price might keep customers from buying a product.	——	——	——
5. It is best to set a price in the middle of the "acceptable range."	——	——	——

[Now, listen to the speaker.]

Compare your answers with an associate. Then, while you are listening the second time, take brief notes to help you answer the following questions.

LEARNING STRATEGY

Managing Your Learning: Taking notes while you listen gives you a useful reference for future review.

1. What are some methods of getting input from your customers?
2. What is the "expected range"?
3. What is the "acceptable range"?
4. What is the second part to this old saying: "There are two fools in every market . . ."?

Compare your answers in a business team. Then discuss and answer the following questions.

1. What is the difference between expected range and acceptable range?
2. The speaker says that "It is important to realize that the ranges have not just a top end, but a bottom end as well." What are some reasons that people would not buy a product priced too low?
3. In your opinion, is it best to price at the top, the bottom, or in the middle of your target market's acceptable range? Why?

J. PUTTING IT ALL TOGETHER: HOW HIGH CAN YOU GO?

In a business team, decide on the right price for a new product. Read through the following steps before you begin the activity.

1. Decide on your team's product or service. You can begin brainstorming by sharing the product ideas you came up with for your marketing partnership proposal in Part I, Exercise D, page 93, and also for your promotion preparation sheet in Part II, Exercise H, page 102.
2. Decide what you think people would expect to pay for your product or service.
3. Decide what you think people in your target market will be willing to pay for your product or service.
4. Finally, conduct a survey. Each team member will briefly interview three to five people who fit your target market. You will describe your product or service for them, then ask the following questions:
   • Would you consider buying it?

   NOTE If the answer is "No" to this question, the interviewee is disqualified from the survey, and you will have to find someone else.

   • What would you *expect* the highest price for this product to be?
   • What would you expect the lowest price for it to be?
   • What is the highest price *you* would pay for this product?
   • What is the lowest you would pay and still feel it was a quality product?

> **Threads**
>
> **Cutting prices is usually insanity if the competition can go as low as you can.**
>
> Michael Porter, *Newsweek*

Now, use the Pricing Proposal form below to organize the material for your interview.

PRICING PROPOSAL

Product Description:

_____

_____

_____

_____

_____

_____

_____

_____

Question	Team Estimate	Survey Results
Highest Expected Price?	_____	_____
Lowest Expected Price?	_____	_____
Highest Acceptable Price?	_____	_____
Lowest Acceptable Price?	_____	_____
Team's Proposed Price:	_____	

PART III

Evaluation

How well did you achieve the objectives for this chapter? List your results. Use the prompts that accompany each objective.

OBJECTIVES	RESULTS
Business 1. To learn about the "4 Ps" of marketing 2. To discover how new marketing strategies reflect the current needs of today's consumer 3. To predict consumer needs and create a marketing plan that meets them 4. To evaluate various promotional strategies and determine how efficient they will be in reaching target markets 5. To develop your own plans for successfully marketing a product	**Business** 1. Write brief sentences telling something you learned about each of the "4 Ps"— (1) product, (2) place/distribution, (3) promotion, and (4) price. 2. Briefly describe some current consumer needs. Then describe a marketing method that meets those needs. 3. Briefly describe the ordering system from your "Showroom Proposal"—Part II, Exercise D, pages 98–99—and explain why it will meet consumer needs. 4. Give an example of a current promotional strategy. Briefly explain why you think the strategy will succeed or fail in reaching its target market. 5. Describe a product and marketing plan that you have developed while working on this chapter.
Language 6. To understand and be able to use words and expressions related to the topic of marketing 7. To describe how a marketing plan works, using *by*-phrases 8. To improve your English conversation skills by conducting out-of-class interviews	**Language** 6. List four new terms you have learned related to the topic of marketing, and write a brief definition for each. 7. Write three sentences that describe how a marketing method works using the *by*-phrase structure. 8. Describe something you have learned about your ability to converse in English while conducting your interview outside of class.
Personal _____ _____ _____	**Personal** _____ _____ _____

Now answer the following questions:

• What are your strengths in the area of marketing?
• How can you continue to learn about marketing on your own?

Investing in High Tech

CHAPTER PREVIEW

In this chapter, you'll

Threads

William H. Gates III,
CEO of Microsoft
Corporation, launched
the company at the age
of 19, after dropping out
of Harvard.

*Louis Rukeyser's Business
Almanac*

- discover how the stock market in the United States operates.
- understand high-tech investment advice.
- learn how to read stock market listings in the newspaper and familiarize yourself with the *Wall Street Journal*.
- practice understanding and giving advice.
- understand and be able to use words and expressions related to the topic of high-tech investing.

> <u>October</u>. *This is one of the peculiarly dangerous months to speculate in stocks in. The others are July, January, September, April, November, May, March, June, December, August, and February.*
>
> —Mark Twain (Samuel Langhorne Clemens), 1835–1910, American author and riverboat captain. From *Pudd'nhead Wilson's Calendar.*

Investors in high tech can win big or lose big. Whether they win or lose, they usually make investment decisions based on advice from a variety of sources. This chapter includes information and advice from the same sources experienced investors use—you'll learn about playing the stock market in general and about investing in high-tech stocks in particular.

PART I

Preparation

LEARNING STRATEGY

Forming Concepts: Sharing what you already know about something helps you understand new information on the topic.

A. BRAINSTORMING

With your business team, look at the photo, and discuss your answers to the questions that follow.

- Companies such as IBM, Apple, Hewlett Packard, Sharp, Intel, and Microsoft bring us products like those in the photo. What are some other high-tech companies and products you are familiar with?
- Which of these companies are particularly successful right now? *Why* are they successful?
- How do you know that a corporation is successful?
- Which of these companies would you invest money in? Why?
- What do you know about the stock market in the United States?

B. WORKING WITH CONCEPTS: COMPUTER STOCKS

Following is an excerpt of an article on investing in computer stocks from *U.S. News and World Report,* dated July 26, 1993. Before you read it, discuss the answers to these questions:

1. How well were computer stocks doing in the summer of 1993?
2. How well are they doing now?

Computer stocks

by Jack Egan

Betting on computer stocks has always been a great way for investors to make, and lose, money. Lately, it's mainly been the latter. While analysts attribute some of the recent price weakness to seasonal factors—for some reason, computer shares often slump during the dog days of summer—the carnage has been especially gruesome over the past several weeks as the PC price wars heat up.

Last week, the stock of Dell Computer, the leader in direct-mail marketing of PCs, plunged more than 15 percent to under $16 after the company announced its first-ever quarterly loss. The stock has been on a slippery downslope since it peaked in early 1993 at just under $50.

But Dell's drop was a prelude to the hard hit taken by Apple Computer. After announcing a new round of drastic price cuts, Apple stunned analysts by reporting a record loss for its third quarter. The shares lost $9.25 for the

week, closing at $27.50, a 2 1/2-year low. At that price the stock does have some advocates like Michael Murphy, editor of the *California Technology Stock Letter,* who is aggressively recommending purchase because of its "international franchise and the large number of new products Apple's about to launch." But new Apple CEO Michael Spindler will face a skeptical bunch when he appears before Wall Street analysts this week. "Lopping off a few heads and dropping product prices are meaningful and correct first steps," observes David Wu of S.G. Warburg & Co., who is reserving judgment, "but they are only the beginning of what's required to get the company back on track." The same goes for battered IBM, whose stock closed last week at $54.63, a new 12-month low. "If you don't own IBM stock now, there's no sense in rushing into it," advises Wu. At least two more quarters of losses and the likelihood of another dividend cut are hanging over what some are now calling Big Black and Blue.

The only major PC maker considered a clear winner is Compaq Computer. Wu

recommends this stock, along with shares of Intel and Advanced Micro Devices, which produce chips. He's also high on workstation maker Sun Microsystems and Novell, which manufactures software to link networks of PCs. Compaq has become the world's most cost-efficient producer of PCs, so that even Taiwanese PC giants like Acer are dropping out of the desktop business "because they can't compete with Compaq," says Harry Lange, portfolio manager for the Fidelity Select Computer mutual fund. Compaq is the biggest holding in Lange's fund. The next-largest holding is Silicon Graphics, which has carved out a niche by making high-end graphics workstations. The company, whose computers helped produce some of the special effects in the film "Jurassic Park," is about to introduce a multimedia workstation aggressively priced at around $5,000. Silicon Graphics stock was trading at about $38 a share last week, close to its 1993 high.

Adapted from "Computer Stocks: Avoiding the Slide," by Jack Egan. U.S. News and World Report, July 26, 1993. Pp. 52–53.

C. JARGON, BUZZWORDS, AND SLANG: STOCK MARKET TALK

Stock prices go up and down. Which of these terms from the article describe the "ups"? Which describe the "downs"? Check the correct column for each term.

IT WORKS!
Learning Strategy:
Classifying New
Words

	UP ↑	DOWN ↓
• to slump	_____	_____
• to plunge	_____	_____
• to peak	_____	_____
• a downslope	_____	_____
• a drop	_____	_____
• a high	√	_____
• a low	_____	_____
• _____	_____	_____
• _____	_____	_____
• _____	_____	_____

Threads

In 1792, 24 brokers in New York City formed the first stock market in America under a buttonwood tree at what is now 68 Wall Street.

Louis Rukeyser's Business Almanac

In the remaining spaces, add any other words you can think of that describe stock market ups and downs.

Now test your knowledge of these stock terms from the article by using them to complete the crossword puzzle. The answers are on page 114.

mutual fund   invest   Wall Street
portfolio   quarter   close
share   dividend

Across

1. A collection of stocks an individual chooses to invest in
2. A unit of ownership
3. A 3-month period of time in which businesses calculate profits and losses
4. A collection of stocks and/or bonds an investment company selects for people to invest in
5. Money some companies pay to shareholders on a regular basis

Down

1. The financial district in New York City
2. To buy shares in a company
3. To be at the final stock price on a given day

LEARNING STRATEGY

Forming Concepts: Applying new information to real-world situations makes a topic easier to understand.

D. PUTTING IT ALL TOGETHER

Re-read "Computer Stocks: Avoiding the Slide." Working with your business team, complete the following chart on some of the stock winners and losers mentioned in the article. To do this, you'll use information in the article, but since it appeared in July 1993, you'll need to get additional information in one of the following ways:

- Ask an associate.
- Look in today's paper.
- Go to or call the business reference librarian at your school or community library.
- Go to or call the librarian at a special business library, if you have one in your community.

Stock Losers

COMPANY	PRODUCT	CLOSING STOCK PRICE AS OF JULY '93	CURRENT STOCK PRICE

Stock Winners

COMPANY	PRODUCT	CLOSING STOCK PRICE AS OF JULY '93	CURRENT STOCK PRICE

Now list additional high-tech companies that are doing well in today's market:

COMPANY	PRODUCT	CURRENT STOCK PRICE

(Crossword puzzle)

Down/Across answers:
¹w a l l s t r e e t
²i n v e s t
³c o s t
¹p o r t f o l i o
s h a r e
³q u a r t e r
⁴m u t u a l f u n d
⁵d i v i d e n d

E. DEBRIEFING MEETING

Compare your business team's findings with those of other business teams. Discuss which high-tech companies you would invest in right now, and why.

F. SETTING OBJECTIVES

Following are the goals for this chapter. Read them, and consider your personal goals. At the end of this chapter, on page 126, you'll list your results.

OBJECTIVES

Business
1. To discover how the stock market in the United States operates
2. To understand high-tech investment advice
3. To learn why some high-tech companies do well in a recession, while others suffer
4. To learn how to read stock market listings in the newspaper
5. To familiarize yourself with the *Wall Street Journal*

Language
6. To practice understanding and giving advice
7. To understand and be able to use words and expressions related to the topics of high-tech investing and the stock market
8. To be able to describe events in the recent past using the present perfect with *for* and *since*

Personal

_____

_____

_____

Integration

A. SUCCESS AT SHARP: A CASE STUDY

Following is an article on the Japanese high-tech company, Sharp. Articles like this present background information on business successes and failures so readers can make informed investment decisions. They appear in magazines and periodicals such as *Fortune, Barrons, Business Week,* and the *Wall Street Journal.* This article, from the March 23, 1992 issue of *Fortune,* explains how Sharp's stock stayed high in the early 90s despite the consumer electronics recession.

Before you read the selection, discuss these questions with your business team, and write out your answers.

1. What do you know about Sharp? What are its best known products?
2. How is the company doing right now?

Sharp: From technology to market—first

by Sally Soto

The world according to Sharp: Master a technology; mold it into products so useful that even the most gadget-averse consumers can't resist; repeat.

The Japanese consumer electronics maverick is the world's largest supplier of liquid crystal displays, which first illuminated calculators and are now lighting up sales of electronic organizers, the gizmos that store phone numbers, appointments, memos, you name it. Sharp plans to use the technology to hang a flat TV on your wall and put a computer in your pocket.

Less than a quarter the size of its Osaka neighbor Matsushita, and not half as big as glamorous compatriot Sony, Sharp has forged a path all its own. The secret? Sharp is, well, sharp at keeping one eye on research, the other on the ever-changing consumer. The reward? In the fiscal year that ends March 31, Boris Petersik, analyst at

Barclays de Zoete Wedd in Tokyo, figures that operating income will fall only 10%—not bad in a consumer electronics recession when rivals' profits will drop further or disappear.

Although RCA was experimenting in the 1960s with LCDs, made by sealing liquid crystal between sheets of glass, Sharp designed one into a calculator in 1973. The company has since put the screens on portable computers, mini–color TVs, projectors, and more. It claimed a 38% share of the $2.1 billion world market for LCDs in 1991, a business expected to hit $7.1 billion in 1995.

The Wizard, a 10-ounce, 7-by-3.7-inch organizer based on displays and semiconductors developed for Sharp calculators, began as a product of the Personal Home/Office Electronics Division, fondly called "Phoo-ey." Says Gil DeLiso, now head of the division that markets it in the U.S: "We saw that lifestyles were becoming busier. People had more information to manage." The gadget, aimed at business travelers, was introduced in 1988.

Bingo. Sales approached $400 million last year. Says Richard Shaffer, editor of *ComputerLetter:* "Sharp essentially created a market that others dismissed as toys. Computer makers think everything is an office machine. The big payoff comes in finding a machine for people who say no to the question 'Do you need a computer?'" A dedicated sales force is trying to get companies to say yes to Wizards with software customized for their traveling salesmen and such. Among the takers: Prudential Property & Casualty Insurance and PepsiCo.

Sharp's keen take on U.S. consumers has made it No. 1 in fax machines and microwaves. In the mid-1980s it foresaw a big reception for faxing when competitors saw only a niche for what were exotic, expensive devices. Sharp scaled down a model to fit standard $8\frac{1}{2}$-by-11-inch American paper. Japanese paper is larger. It lowered the price below $2,000, and the boom on rivals. Sales quadrupled in 1987 to 100,000 units and have more than tripled since. In microwaves, Sharp was first with a sensor for popcorn popping.

The company's American surge came largely under Toshikazu Mitsuda, 56, until recently chairman of the $2.2-billion-a-year U.S. subsidiary. Mitsuda, now head of European operations, hit the road often, making unannounced calls on dealers: "I saw how they treated customers. I got their honest feelings about Sharp. Chocolate never helps. Bitter medicine does."

Sharp's next breakthrough product could be wall-hanging TVs. The latest is 8.6 inches diagonally and costs about $4,800. But the company's three-year, $714 million investment in LCD research aims to make the devices bigger and cheaper. Robert Garbutt, head of the LCD division in the U.S., notes that in the past year the clarity of an LCD picture closed in on that of today's standard, bulkier cathode ray tubes.

Sharp is also about to apply itself to a new technology called "flash" semiconductors. In February it signed an agreement with Intel to develop and manufacture the reprogrammable chips, which retain information stored in them even when the power is turned off. The company believes flash chips will boost development of smaller and more powerful portable computers, say, Wizard-size ones. Says Richard Pashley, general manager of Intel's memory components division: "We're expecting the flash market to explode"—to $2 billion in 1995, from $130 million last year. Sharp, he predicts, will lead the push into consumer applications.

From "Technology to Market—First," by Sally Soto. Fortune, March 23, 1992. P. 108.

LEARNING STRATEGY

Forming Concepts: Analyzing what you've read sharpens your critical thinking skills.

B. ANALYZING WHAT YOU'VE READ

Threads

As of 1994, Sharp Corporation had 43% of the worldwide liquid crystal display (LCD) market, twice that of their nearest competitor.

Stanford Resource

IT WORKS!
Learning Strategy:
Applying New
Information to Real-
World Situations

With your business team, answer the following questions about the passage you just read and write out your answers.

1. What technology is Sharp best known for? What percent of the world market share does Sharp have for products incorporating this technology?
2. What gadget created by Sharp increased that company's profits and helped them avoid the high-tech slump?
3. What two other very successful product lines has Sharp been heavily involved in?
4. List the two products Sharp intends to come out with in the near future.
5. Come to a consensus opinion—a group decision—regarding Sharp's formula for success. Write your team's opinion on a sheet of paper.
6. This article was written in the spring of 1992. How is Sharp doing today? With your business team, do research to complete the following grid with current facts about Sharp. Get the information, using one or more of the following:
   • Ask an associate.
   • Look in today's paper. (Sharp is on the Tokyo stock exchange—look for "Foreign Markets.")
   • Go to the business section of your school or community library and look for articles on Sharp in current business publications.

SHARP
New products currently on the market:
Plans for future products:
Current stock price:
Other facts about the company:

Now, answer this question with your business team:

- Is Sharp still a good investment? Why or Why not?

C. JARGON, BUZZWORDS, AND SLANG: BUSINESS JOURNALISM JARGON

Rewrite the following statements taken from the article "Sharp: Technology to Market—First." Replace the underlined expressions with their journalistic jargon equivalents from the list:

keen take on	keeping an eye on
lowered the boom on	forged a path
hit the road	payoff

1. Sharp's <u>excellent understanding of</u> U.S. consumers has made it No. 1 in fax machines and microwaves.
2. Mitsuda, now head of European operations, <u>traveled</u> often, making unannounced calls on dealers.
3. Sharp is, well, *sharp* at <u>closely watching</u> research and the ever-changing consumer.
4. It lowered the price below $2,000, and <u>eliminated</u> its competition.
5. Less than a quarter the size of its Osaka neighbor Matsushita, and not half as big as glamorous compatriot Sony, Sharp <u>has created a place in the market</u> all its own.
6. The big <u>reward</u> comes in finding a machine for people who say no to the question, "Do you need a computer?"

LEARNING STRATEGY

Forming New Concepts: Studying a grammar point in the context of a topic you're studying helps you learn it faster.

Communication Memo • Communication Memo • Communication Memo

To: All Employees
From: Corporate Communications Department
Re: The present perfect tense with *for* and *since*

Because people often use the present perfect tense when they discuss the stock market, please review our corporate rules on the use of this form with *for* and *since:*

Review: One use of the present perfect tense is to describe an activity that started in the past and has continued into the present. When you want to state the time frame the activity took place in, you use a time expression such as "three years" or "last week", with *for* or *since*.

<u>For</u>

You use *for* with a time expression that refers to a **duration,** as in this example:
• The stock has been on a slippery slope <u>for the last nine months</u>.

<u>Since</u>

You use *since* with a time expression that refers to a **point in time,** as in this example:
• The stock has been on a slippery slope <u>since it peaked in April 1993</u>.

Note the different ways to refer to **duration** and **points in time:**

Duration	**Point in Time**
for the last three quarters	since last year
for a long time	since he joined the company
for many years	since the last election

Please fill out the enclosed attachment and return it to your department head.

Enc.
CM/lb

Memo Attachment

Read the following groups of phrases. On a sheet of paper, put each one into a complete sentence using *for* or *since* and the present perfect.

EXAMPLES   The stock/be on a slippery slope/the last nine months → The stock has been on a slippery slope for the last nine months.

Sharp's stock/to increase/it announced its new product → Sharp's stock has increased since it announced its new product.

1. Dell's stock/to plunge/the company announced its first-ever quarterly loss
2. Sharp/to forge a path all its own/the company was founded
3. Sharp/to put LCD screens on portable computers/the last ten years
4. Sales/to quadruple/last quarter
5. Robert Garbutt/to be head of the LCD division/many years
6. Mr. Mitsuda/to be in Japan/the last three weeks

D. PUTTING IT ALL TOGETHER

Working with your business team, find a company whose profits have dropped recently. (It *can* be, but doesn't *have* to be, a high-tech company.) Following the example of Sharp, make suggestions for exciting, innovative new products that might stimulate profits for this company. Use your imagination, but base your ideas on existing technology.

NOTE You may also suggest any other strategies you can think of that would help this company increase profits.

Summarize your suggestions on the worksheet below.

STRATEGIES FOR INCREASING PROFITS FOR _____
(company name)

Major product lines:

_____

_____

_____

Current stock price:

_____

Ideas for new products:

_____

_____

_____

_____

Additional strategies for increasing profits:

_____

_____

_____

_____

Other facts about the company:

_____

_____

_____

_____

When you have finished, role-play the following situation with an associate: One of you plays the role of the head of the Research and Development department of the company your team chose; the other is the CEO of the company.

Present your new product ideas. Include an explanation of how these products will improve company profits. The CEO isn't sure it's worth the expense to develop these new products. The R&D head tries to convince him or her.

Perform the role-play for the other members of your business team. Then evaluate how the R&D head and the CEO communicated, using the following chart. Check whether you thought your associates' form, tone, and nonverbal behavior were appropriate or inappropriate. Then give comments and suggestions to your associates for each feature.

ASSOCIATE A (R&D HEAD)

FEATURE	APPROPRIATE	INAPPROPRIATE	COMMENTS AND SUGGESTIONS
Form			
Tone			
Nonverbal behavior			

ASSOCIATE B (CEO)

FEATURE	APPROPRIATE	INAPPROPRIATE	COMMENTS AND SUGGESTIONS
Form			
Tone			
Nonverbal behavior			

E. FOLLOWING THE STOCK MARKET

Let's say you've heard about a high-tech company that's about to launch an exciting new product. If you'd like to add stock in this company to your investment portfolio, you'll want to follow the growth or decline of your stock on one of the stock exchange listings in the newspaper.

You are going to practice looking for information on one of the three major exchanges in the United States. Before you start, answer the following questions with your business team, writing your answers on a sheet of paper.

- What are the three major exchanges in the United States?
- Give the name of one company and its products (or services) that appears on each of the three exchanges.

Stocks that are issued by newer or smaller companies usually appear on the NASDAQ exchange. Since many high-tech companies appear on this exchange, take a look at the typical example of a NASDAQ listing from the *Wall Street Journal* on Wednesday, September 29, 1993. Below it is an excerpt from a feature called "Explanatory Notes." "Explanatory Notes" helps you read the stock market listings.

NASDAQ NATIONAL MARKET ISSUES

Quotations as of 4 p.m. Eastern Time
Wednesday, September 29, 1993

	52 Weeks Hi	Lo	Stock	Sym	Div	Yld %	PE	Vol 100s	Hi	Lo	Close	Net Chg
						-A-A-A-						
					*	*	*					
	35¾	17¾	AnlyInt	ANLY	.60	1.9	18	81	31½	31¾	31⅞	+⅝
	3⅝	1	Anaren	ANEN		...	50	39	3⅜	3	3	...
	15⅛	5¾	AnchrBcp	ABKR		...	6	588	14⅜	14	14⅛	+⅛
	24¾	13¾	AnchrBcpWis	ABCW	.18e	.8	...	109	24	23¼	23¼	...
	19⅝	5¾	AndovrBcp	ANDB	.05e	.3	8	503	19⅝	19	19	−⅛
	4⅜	1¾	AndovrTog	ATOG		...	13	33	1¾	1¾	1¾	...
S▲	39	16½	AndrewCp	ANDW		...	25	1635	39¼	38¼	38¼	−½
	19¼	10⅞	Andros	ANDY		...	12	171	15¼	14¾	14⅞	−⅛
	13½	**5⅕**	**Anergen**	**ANRG**		**...**	**...**	**96**	**7**	**6¼**	**7**	**+¾**
n▲	25	21	ANTEC Cp	ANTC		...	...	6192	25½	23½	24¾	+¾
	5⅝	**1¾**	**ApertusTech**	**APTS**		**...**	**20**	**1909**	**3¼**	**2⅝**	**3¼**	**+5/16**
	14¼	9¾	ApogeeEnt	APOG	.28	2.2	30	94	12¾	12¼	12⅝	+⅜
	65¼	23½	AppleCptr	AAPL	.48	2.0	17	21138	24⅞	23¾	23⅞	−⅞
S	21	5¼	AppleSouth	APSO	.02	.1	53	314	20½	19¾	20	−⅛
S	22¾	9⅞	Applebee	APPB		...	43	344	22¼	21¾	22⅛	−⅛
	20	7¾	ApplncRecyc	ARCI		...	dd	4	11	11	11	+½
	14	4½	AppldBiosci	APBI		...	53	1512	5⅞	5¾	5⅞	+⅛
	2¼	⅞	AppliedCrbn	ACTYF		...	...	135	1⅜	1⅜	1⅜	...
	7	4¼	ApplдExtr	AETC		...	59	42	5⅞	5⅞	5⅞	...
	25¼	11	ApplдImuSci	AISX		...	...	1465	14⅜	14	14	−⅜
▲	**78¾**	**24**	**ApplдMatl**	**AMAT**		**...**	**38**	**13526**	**80**	**72**	**72⅞**	**−5⅝**
n	**8¼**	**4¼**	**ApplдSignal**	**APSG**		**...**	**...**	**169**	**5¼**	**4½**	**4½**	**−½**
	5⅜	**2⅛**	**ArabShld**	**ARSD**		**...**	**...**	**10**	**2¼**	**2¼**	**2¼**	**−⅛**
					*	*	*					
	25¾	9¾	AtlTeleNtwk	ATNI	40	3.5	14	37	12	11½	11½	−¼
	38⅝	10½	Atmel	ATML		...	35	4340	37¾	36⅝	37	−⅜
▼	10½	6¼	AtrixLabs	ATRX		...	...	3216	6¾	5¾	6½	−⅛
	11½	8½	AtwoodOcn	ATWD		...	dd	6	10½	10½	10½	+¼
	29	16½	AuBonPain A	ABPCA		...	43	1766	21	20	20½	+½
	6⅜	2 15/16	AuraSystems	AURA		...	dd	1240	5½	5⅜	5⅜	...
n	15½	9¾	AuspexSys	ASPX		...	...	943	11½	11	11¼	...
	16½	9⅛	Autocam	ACAM	.52t	3.5	16	210	15	14½	15	+⅝

Excerpted from *Wall Street Journal,* September 29, 1993.

EXPLANATORY NOTES

The following explanations apply to New York and American exchange listed issues and the National Association of Securities Dealers Automated Quotations system's over-the-counter securities. Exchange prices are composite quotations that include trades on the Chicago, Pacific, Philadelphia, Boston and Cincinnati exchanges and reported by the NASD.

Boldfaced quotations highlight those issues whose price changed by 5% or more if their previous closing price was $2 or higher.

Underlined quotations are those stocks with large changes in volume, per exchange, compared with the issue's average trading volume. The calculation includes common stocks of $5 a share or more with an average volume over 65 trading days of at least 5,000 shares. The underlined quotations are for the 40 largest volume percentage leaders on the NYSE and NASD's National Market System. It includes the 20 largest volume percentage gainers on the Amex.

The 52-week high and low columns show the highest and lowest price on the issue during the preceding 52 weeks plus the current week, but not the latest trading day. These ranges are adjusted to reflect stock payouts of 4% or more, and cash dividends of 10% or more.

Dividend rates, unless noted, are annual disbursements based on the last quarterly, semiannual, or annual declaration. Special or extra dividends, special situations or payments not designated as regular are identified by footnotes.

Yield is defined as the dividends paid by a company on its securities, expressed as a percentage of price.

The P/E ratio is determined by dividing the closing market price by the company's primary per-share earnings for the most recent four quarters. Charges and other adjustments usually are excluded when they qualify as extraordinary items under generally accepted accounting rules.

Sales figures are the unofficial daily total of shares traded, quoted in hundreds (two zeros omitted).

Exchange ticker symbols are shown for all New York and American exchange common stocks, and Dow Jones News/Retrieval symbols are listed for Class A and Class B shares listed on both markets. Nasdaq symbols are listed for all Nasdaq NMS issues. A more detailed explanation of Nasdaq ticker symbols appears with the NMS listings.

Excerpted from *Wall Street Journal,* September 29, 1993.

F. ANALYZING WHAT YOU'VE READ

Practice finding stock market information by answering the following questions on a sheet of paper about the NASDAQ stock listings and the Explanatory Notes.

1. Find the listing for Apple Computer. How is the company name abbreviated? Write it. Next to its name is the company's ticker symbol. It's written in capital letters. Write Apple's ticker symbol.
2. What was Apple's highest stock price on Wednesday, September 29, 1993? What was it's lowest price? At what price did it close that day?
3. Find a stock in the listing that closed at a higher price than Apple on that day. Write the company name and the closing price of the stock.
4. Find a stock that closed at a lower price than Apple and write its name and closing price.
5. Why is Apertus Tech (Apertus Technology) written in boldface type?
6. Why is AtrixLabs underlined?
7. Explain in your own words what a P/E ratio is, and list Apple's and Apertus's PEs.

LEARNING STRATEGY

Overcoming Limitations: Guessing the meaning of new words helps you become an independent learner.

G. JARGON, BUZZWORDS, AND SLANG: STOCK TALK

Find the following stock market terms in the "Explanatory Notes" and underline them. With an associate, find out what each term means. Write the definitions in the column on the right.

Terms	Definitions
trades	_____
an issue	_____
a gainer	_____
a payout (also a disbursement)	_____
exchange ticker symbols	_____

LEARNING STRATEGY

Managing Your Learning: Turning a learning activity into a game helps you learn new material quickly and easily.

H. PUTTING IT ALL TOGETHER: THE *WALL STREET JOURNAL*

Bring a current issue of the *Wall Street Journal* to class. With your business team, find the following information. Be the first team to find all the information, then share your findings in a company meeting.

1. What kind of information do you find in the first section (Section A) of the paper?
2. What section contains information on the stock market?
3. Look in the "Money & Investing" section of the paper (Section C) for a column entitled "Stock Market Data Bank." What kind of information does this feature contain?
   a. List the most active issues on the following exchanges: NYSE; NASDAQ; AMEX.
   b. List the greatest price percentage gainer on the following exchanges: NYSE; NASDAQ; AMEX.
4. Find the Stock Market Index box in the "World Markets" section and answer these questions:
   a. What is the percent change for: Tokyo Nikkei? Zurich Swiss Market? Madrid General Index?
   b. Which exchange gained the most? Which lost the most?
5. Still in the Money & Investing section, find today's U.S. dollar equivalent for: Chilean peso; Brazilian cruzeiro; Finland markka.
6. In a column called "Grains and Feeds," find the cash price of oats today. Find the cash price of barley one year ago.
7. What kind of advertising do you find in this section of the *Wall Street Journal*? List some of the companies that advertise and the services they provide.

I. LISTENING TO STOCK MARKET INFORMATION

You can hear stock market information on daily radio and TV programs such as "The Nightly Business Report" on PBS TV and "Marketplace" on National Public Radio. Following is an excerpt from "The Nightly Business Report." Listen to the report one time and, on a sheet of paper, jot down the names of any high-tech companies that you recognize.

Now, listen again and answer these questions:

1. What industry's stock prices all went down?
2. Which company's losses does the announcer say affected this whole group?

Now, listen to the broadcast again, as many times as you want, and answer the following questions.

HINT Read the following questions before you listen again.

1. What do the following companies do?
   a. Advanced Micro Devices
   b. Micron Technology
   c. Applied Materials

Threads

The highest paid investment consultant in the world is Harry D. Shultz, whose consultation fee is $2,400 per hour.

Guinness Book of Records, 1993

2. Indicate whether the following companies' stock was up or down on the day of this broadcast (Circle the correct answer):

National Semiconductor	UP	DOWN
IBM	UP	DOWN
Intel	UP	DOWN
Microsoft	UP	DOWN
Oracle	UP	DOWN

J. PUTTING IT ALL TOGETHER

Look in newspapers or business magazines for new high-tech companies or products that are coming on the market. Imagine that you have $150,000 to invest in the stock market, and choose one or more high-tech companies that interest you. Make a company-wide consensus decision as to how long you will follow your investments. Follow your investments for the time allotted, and then report on your earnings (or losses) in a company meeting.

To prepare for your report, record the investment information for each company you invest in. Including the following:

- price per share
- the number of shares you bought
- your total investment
- the selling price and your earnings or losses

(You can use the following chart, if you wish.)

Threads

There are more important things in life than a little money, and one of them is a lot of money.

Anonymous

INVESTMENT RECORD
Name of company:
Exchange:
Ticker symbol:
Price per share (as of buy date):
Number of shares you bought:
Total investment:
Selling price (as of date you decided on):
Earnings/Losses:

Evaluation

How well did you achieve the objectives for this chapter? List your results on a sheet of paper. Use the prompts that accompany each objective.

OBJECTIVES	RESULTS
Business 1. To discover how the stock market in the United States operates 2. To understand high-tech investment advice 3. To learn why some high-tech companies do well in a recession, while others suffer 4. To learn how to read stock market listings in the newspaper 5. To familiarize yourself with the *Wall Street Journal*	**Business** 1. Write a brief explanation of how the market operates. 2. Give one example of high-tech investing advice that you discovered in this chapter. 3. Give one example of a high-tech company that did well in a recent recession, and explain why this happened. 4. List the three main exchanges in the United States, and give an example of a high-tech company that trades on each. 5. List three things that you can find in the Money & Investing section of the *Wall Street Journal.*
Language 6. To practice understanding and giving advice 7. To understand and be able to use words and expressions related to the topics of high-tech investing and the stock market 8. To be able to describe events in the recent past using the present perfect with *for* and *since*	**Language** 6. Write a statement in which you give investment advice. 7. Write three new buzzwords or expressions you learned in this chapter. 8. Write a sentence about one of the stocks you bought in Part II, Exercise J, page 124, using *for* or *since* and the present perfect.
Personal _____ _____ _____	**Personal** _____ _____ _____

Now, answer the following questions:

• What are your strengths in the area of investing in high tech?
• How can you continue to learn about high-tech investing on your own?

Environmental Issues in Business

In this chapter you'll

- learn how environmental issues impact business.
- research controversial environmental issues.
- learn about "environmentally responsible" business programs and products.
- analyze corporate and consumer concerns regarding environmental issues.
- effectively express an argument using appropriate transition words and phrases.

We need to take a broader, more integrated look at the range of environmental programs available to us, with an eye toward finding the most efficient and effective way to reduce risk.

—William K. Reilly, Environmental Protection Agency Administrator

In recent years growing public concern regarding environmental matters has caused many businesses to rethink their stand on environmental issues and to adopt environmentally responsible policies. In this chapter, you will learn about current environmental issues and evaluate the arguments for and against them. You will find out how today's businesses and environmental groups are working together to find creative solutions to environmental problems. You will also research some of the unique products and services that environmental issues have inspired in the business world.

PART I

Preparation

A. BRAINSTORMING

Work with an associate. Look at the opening photo and on a sheet of paper, write your answers to the following questions.

- List advantages to companies that obey environmental laws and take voluntary action to be "environmentally responsible."
- List reasons why companies are sometimes against environmental laws.

- When there are costs involved in obeying these laws, who is responsible for the expense?
- When there is disagreement about an environmental law, how are the controversies usually solved?

B. WORKING WITH CONCEPTS: ENVIRONMENTAL LEGISLATION IN BUSINESS

The following articles are about federal and local environmental laws that have caused debates between environmentalists and businesses. Before you read, form a business team to discuss how to deal with the following situations. Write your answers on a sheet of paper.

LEARNING STRATEGY

Overcoming Limitations: Discussing controversial situations in English improves your ability to speak clearly and express your views accurately.

1. Imagine you recently purchased property that you plan to use for business. Yesterday, you received an order from the government stating that your property is contaminated with toxic wastes and you must pay for the cleanup process before you can operate your business. List your possible resolutions to this situation.
2. You own a restaurant that does a lot of "to-go" business. Recently, your city council passed a law forbidding the use of polystyrene foam containers because they are an environmental hazard. So, you are now giving discounts to people who bring their own to-go containers, even if they are made of polystyrene. The town council and some of your competitors are upset at this practice and want you to attend a council meeting to discuss it. List solutions that might satisfy all of you.
3. Imagine it is against U.S. federal law to smoke in public places. You are a manager in a large hotel hosting a major international convention that will generate a great deal of revenue. You have been informed that many of the conventioneers will want to smoke, so you reserve additional "smoking areas" around the hotel. Consequently, several staff members have refused to work during the convention, saying that they will be unlawfully exposed to hazardous working conditions. How will you resolve this situation?

Threads

Small-business owners will need financial and technical assistance to help them afford the pollution prevention equipment and understand their obligations under new laws.

Richard Herring, chair of National Small Business United's legislative committee

Article 1

Superfund: Environmental cleanup laws have released a flood of lawsuits

by Shannon Henry

Superfund, otherwise known as the Comprehensive Environmental Response, Compensation, and Liability Act, was created in 1980 to identify and clean up the most hazardous sites in the United States. Under this legislation, owners of contaminated sites first pay for cleanup. Then they go through the legal process of applying for certification that the property is "clean" according to government standards.

To date, only about 60 of the 1,200 Superfund sites on the "National Priority List" have been checked off the list. Because the legal aspects of Superfund are so complicated, the cleanup process has been slowed down by a "litigation flood." There are so many lawsuits because so many people can be held accountable; all parties involved in a contaminated site—buyers and sellers alike—can be drawn into legal battles over Superfund.

Those who support Superfund say it will encourage voluntary cleanup of hundreds of thousands of sites around the country for economic development and job creation. But some analysts say that Superfund will prevent new business investments and is particularly harmful to small businesses. The National Federation of Independent Businesses reports that many of its members have been forced into bankruptcy from the high cleanup costs.

Mary Bernhard, manager of environmental policy at the U.S. Chamber of Commerce, said she gets calls from small-business owners who have just bought land and have discovered that the previous owner left toxic waste behind. "For the small-business guy, once he gets his letter from the Environmental Protection Agency (EPA), declaring his land a Superfund site, the legal bills might be more expensive than the cleanup would be," Bernhard said. "He might then turn around to the EPA and say, 'You've just bought yourself a business.'"

Adapted and excerpted from "Superfund: Environmental Cleanup Laws Have Released a Flood of Lawsuits," by Shannon Henry. Christian Science Monitor, July 2, 1993.

Article 2

Fairfax's ban on plastic foam goes into effect this week

by Diane Curtis

Following the lead of about 60 other communities nationwide, Fairfax, California, will become the first Marin County community to ban polystyrene food packaging for anything prepared in the town. Under the city ordinance approved last month by the Town Council, all businesses with takeout services must use some alternative to the foam cups, plates, and small containers used by most food sellers.

In defense of the measure, Town Administrator Linda Christman said that a litter problem and the low rate of foam recycling were the reasons for the ban. Although polystyrene is recycled to make such products as coat hangers, egg cartons, and insulation, she said it is unlikely that people rushing around with take-out food and drinks will take the trouble to find a recycling bin. "We think that foam is a unique litter problem," she added. "It tends to be persistent; it blows around, it floats, it falls into the creek, it breaks into pieces."

But some business owners are not so enthusiastic about the ban. Anita Dal Porto, co-owner of Java Dal Porto, said she and her partner thoroughly investigated the pros and cons of using foam cups before they opened their restaurant and decided they were the best all-round choice, even environmentally. She argued that the ordinance is illogical. "Let's be real. There's no *paper* litter?" She says it isn't fair that while she is not allowed to serve food or drinks in foam containers, she is allowed to buy foam containers from the town's supermarket and use them herself.

Businesses that do not comply with the ban will face an $80.00 fine.

Adapted and excerpted from "Fairfax's Ban on Plastic Foam Goes into Effect This Week," by Diane Curtis. San Francisco Chronicle, October 12, 1992.

Article 3

Strict public smoking bill has administration support

by Philip J. Hilts

The Clinton Administration yesterday backed legislation to ban smoking in all buildings used by the public, from taverns to hardware stores, saying the nation could save tens of billions of dollars each year, along with 38,000 to 108,000 lives, with only small enforcement costs.

The bill would also ban smoking within the immediate vicinity of the building entrances.

The proposed legislation, the Smoke-Free Environment Act, was debated at a hearing of the Subcommittee on Health and the Environment. It would ban smoking in every building regularly entered by ten or more people at least one day a week, not including residences.

Carol M. Browner, the administrator of the Environmental Protection Agency, testified that her agency estimates that if the bill became law, the lives of 5,000 to 9,000 nonsmokers would be saved, along with those of 33,000 to 99,000 smokers who would quit smoking or cut back.

Browner estimated the savings in medical costs and lost wages at $6.5 billion to $19 billion a year.

The bill provides penalties for those who operate buildings that fail to comply with the law; but it relies on court action by local individuals to enforce the ban.

The bill authorizes any person or agency to take complaints to U.S. District Court, where a fine of up to $5,000 a day could be imposed.

Browner said the cost of enforcement and of "smokers' rooms" in some buildings would amount to $70 million to $200 million a year. She said that if every building in the nation put in a smokers' area, the cost could be as high as $3.5 billion, but she said that would still fall far short of the savings from the measure.

Speaking against the measure was Charles O. Whitley of the Tobacco Institute, which represents large tobacco companies. He said the legislation would waste federal dollars at a great rate because it could lead to numerous legal actions against building owners who failed to enforce the law.

Adapted and excerpted from "Strict Public Smoking Bill Has Administration Support," by Philip J. Hilts. New York Times, February 8, 1994.

C. JARGON, BUZZWORDS, AND SLANG: ENVIRONMENTAL LAW

LEARNING STRATEGY

Remembering New Material: Creating sentences using words and phrases you've just learned helps you remember what they mean.

1. With an associate, look at the picture. Try to make sentences that could describe what is happening in the picture by using the following verb phrases.
   - to hold (someone) accountable
   - to ban
   - to comply with
   - to enforce
   - to impose

2. On a sheet of paper, write full sentences using the following pairs of phrases and the information from the articles you just read.

> *EXAMPLE*   Phrase—<u>to hold accountable/hazardous sites</u>
> Sentence—Under the Superfund law, the government <u>holds</u> companies <u>accountable</u> for cleaning up <u>hazardous sites</u>.

1. to ban/toxic wastes
2. to enforce/legislation
3. to comply/lawsuit
4. to impose/fine

D. PUTTING IT ALL TOGETHER

In a business team, research a controversial environmental law that impacts business now or will impact it in the future. Prepare to report on the issue by answering the following questions on a sheet of paper.

1. Describe the environmental law in question. Be sure to address *who* the law will impact, *how* it will impact them, and *what* the consequences will be for those who do not comply.
2. Who passed or is trying to pass this law? What is the argument in favor of it?
3. Who opposes the law? What is the argument against it?
4. What is your opinion? Gather specific information to support your argument, such as: (a) financial costs; (b) time expenditures; (c) opposing logic. Also, carefully consider the arguments *opposing* your view, so you can debate this issue.

Communication Memo • Communication Memo • Communciation Memo

To:	**All Employees**
From:	**Corporate Communications Department**
Re:	**Transition words expressing contrast and conclusion**

Following is a brief reminder of our corporate rules on using transition words to express contrasting and concluding relationships, which are frequently used in debating an issue.

<u>Expressing Contrast</u>: An effective strategy to use when debating an issue is to first recognize an opposing point, then make a more convincing assertion of your own. To express this kind of relationship, the transition word usually introduces the second, stronger, assertion:

For example: Polystyrene can be recycled. <u>However</u>, it is highly unlikely that busy people will take time to find a recycling bin.

Note the following about this kind of contrast:

- The first statement repeats a probable opposing argument.
- The second statement poses a new argument that makes the argument in the first statement seem less valid, or less logical.

    Other transition words/phrases that express contrast are:
    but   still   on the other hand

    Expressing Conclusion: Another effective debate strategy is to make conclusive statements that show the logic of your argument.
    For example: People can use foam cups outside my restaurant. Therefore, I should be able to use them inside my restaurant.

    Note the following about this kind of conclusion:

- The first statement presents an informative point about the issue.
- The second statement poses a logical argument based on the particular point made in the first statement.

    Other transition words/phrases that express conclusion are:
    so   consequently   as a result

Enc.
CM/ja

Threads

On-Site Toxic Control Inc., of Santa Ana, California, which has developed a new method of cleaning contaminated groundwater, took in around $3 million in 1991.

Forbes, 7/22/91

Memo Attachment

Read the following sentences with an associate. On a sheet of paper, use a transition word or phrase you've just reviewed to begin another sentence that expresses contrast or conclusion. The combination of the two sentences should convey an effective argument.

EXAMPLES Contrast—Superfund was designed to clean up environmentally hazardous sites in the United States. However, few sites have been cleaned up because of high cleanup costs and lawsuits.
Conclusion—For many small businesses, cleanup costs would be so high that they will choose to give up the property. As a result, there will still be many contaminated sites and less investment in commercial property.

1. Conclusion: Individuals and local officials will be responsible for enforcing the Smoke-Free Environment Act.
2. Contrast: There is more litter produced from paper than from polystyrene containers.
3. Contrast: It will cost businesses billions of dollars to add "smokers' rooms."
4. Conclusion: Often, business owners don't know the property they have just bought is a contaminated site.
5. Contrast: Supporters of Superfund say that the cleanup of contaminated sites nationwide will generate jobs.

E. DEBRIEFING

Present your research from Exercise D in a business team meeting. Address each of the points you covered in your preparation. After you have presented your issue and explained your opinion about it, ask your team members for their opinions.

During the discussions and debates among the business teams, evaluate the language and behavior of the participants. Check whether you thought the participants' form, tone, and nonverbal behavior were appropriate or inappropriate. Also jot down brief comments and/or suggestions.

FEATURE	APPROPRIATE	INAPPROPRIATE	COMMENTS AND SUGGESTIONS
Form			
Tone			
Nonverbal behavior			

F. SETTING OBJECTIVES

Following are the goals for this chapter. Read them, and consider your personal goals. At the end of this chapter, on page 146, you'll list your results.

OBJECTIVES

Business
1. To understand how environmental issues impact businesses
2. To research controversial environmental issues and to evaluate both sides of the debate
3. To learn about new methods and programs in business that focus on "environmental responsibility"
4. To analyze corporate motivation in taking steps toward greater environmental responsibility
5. To examine new products and business opportunities that respond to consumers' concern for the environment

Language
6. To practice negotiation and debate strategies
7. To express an argument using appropriate transition words and phrases
8. To be able to use words and expressions related to the topic of environmental issues in business

Personal

_____

_____

_____

Integration

A. MANAGING ENVIRONMENTAL RESPONSIBILITY: DOW CHEMICAL CLEANING UP ITS ACT

The following selection is from an article about a major chemical corporation with a history of fighting government-imposed environmental regulations. In recent years, the company has become more environmentally responsible. Before you read the article, do the following activities with a business team, and write your answers on a sheet of paper.

1. List possible reasons why corporations are now cooperating with environmental agencies instead of resisting them.
2. Give examples of hazardous products or effects produced by chemical companies that environmentalists claim are "environmentally irresponsible."

Dow Chemical cleanup czar unlocks the gates

by John Holusha

Four times a year, David T. Buzzelli, a vice president of the Dow Chemical Company, prepares for a meeting that could have a major impact on the company's operations. To get ready, he gathers information on manufacturing plans and product offerings, including material the company considers confidential.

But this is no ordinary meeting of executives. Instead, Mr. Buzzelli will share the company's plans with a panel of outsiders comprising Dow's Corporate Environmental Advisory Council.

Inviting environmental advocates to examine the way it conducts business is something new for Dow, which in the mid-1980s fought the Environmental Protection Agency all the way to the Supreme Court to prevent airplane inspections of its emissions. But it is typical of the things that have happened since Mr. Buzzelli was named two years ago as the company's first corporate vice president for environmental, health, and safety matters.

Now, Dow has a program in place to cut its key toxic emissions in half by 1995. Plant managers who once ignored anyone beyond the fence are forming community advisory panels and inviting

the neighbors in to see how things are done. And the company has pledged—at least in theory—to phase out products and applications that do not meet environmental standards.

Strong stuff for a company whose best-known product may still be the napalm it produced during the Vietnam War. But Mr. Buzzelli insists that Dow, the nation's second-largest chemical company after Dupont and the maker of such best-selling consumer products as Saran Wrap and Ziploc bags, has changed. The company's future, he says depends on how well it manages its environmental responsibilities and how convincing its efforts are to the public.

"Environment issues are a key factor in the financial success of the company," he said. "We concluded that people who do not pay attention to the environment will not be successful."

People like Mr. Buzzelli are showing up on the organization charts of many top corporations as the complexity and cost of meeting anti-pollution regulations have risen and public concerns about environmental issues have been translated into such laws as the Superfund and Clean Air acts. According to Arthur D. Little, a consulting firm in Cambridge, Mass., 49 of the top 100 manufacturing companies in the country had vice presidents in charge of environmental

affairs in 1991, up from 38 in 1990.

Mr. Buzzelli said Dow has long been concerned about the environment and pollution issues, and points to its relatively small $26 million Superfund liability as evidence. Other companies have liabilities amounting to hundreds of millions of dollars to clean up chemicals and other wastes dumped over the years.

Bringing in environmentalists to comment on the company's products and operations has been a stimulating experience, Mr. Buzzelli admits, particularly for a company that is a major producer of plastics. Plastic products and packaging have been a special target of environmental advocates because they are usually brightly colored and noticeable, are typically used only for a short time, and endure for centuries after disposal.

Nevertheless, Mr. Buzzelli said the process has been useful. In a recent talk to the Midland Rotary Club, Mr. Buzzelli said the Corporate Advisory Council has had a "significant influence on the company. We are hearing things we've never heard before."

Excerpted and adapted from "Dow Chemical Cleanup Czar Unlocks The Gates," by John Holusha. New York Times, September 20, 1992.

Forming Concepts: Making deductions helps you to thoroughly explore a new topic.

B. ANALYZING WHAT YOU'VE READ

With an associate, discuss the following questions about the passage you just read. Write your answers on a sheet of paper.

1. What are Dow Corporation's objectives for meeting with the Environmental Advisory Panel? What do they hope to gain from the meeting?
2. What are the Environmental Advisory Council's objectives in meeting with Dow's executives? What do *they* hope to gain from the meeting?
3. Why has Dow changed its attitude toward environmental regulations—from confrontation in the 1980s, to cooperation in the 1990s?
4. What does Mr. Buzzelli mean when he says that Dow must "convince" the public of its efforts to be environmentally responsible?
5. Explain Buzzelli's logic when he says that, "People who do not pay attention to the environment will not be successful."
6. Read the following excerpt from an article out of *In Business: The Magazine for Environmental Entrepreneuring,* a magazine devoted to environmental issues in business. Then do the activity that follows.

> Eliminating the use of hazardous chemicals is cheaper than disposing of them and accepting the liability for potential spills, and the company's public image is enhanced.
>
> Dow Chemical, for instance, has a program called Waste Reduction Always Pays (WRAP), which recognizes employees who find ways to reduce the firm's output of pollution and hazardous waste. In 1990, the company's top five WRAP projects cut 13.4 million pounds of waste from its manufacturing processes and saved more than $10.5 million.
>
> Another example is Dow's new equipment that separates an organic solvent from water, increasing its recyclability. Consequently, organic solvent waste was reduced by six million pounds, for a savings of $1.2 million a year.
>
> According to the EPA, companies like Union Carbide, 3M, DuPont, Monsanto, General Dynamics, and Northrop also have pollution prevention programs.
>
> Excerpted from "Removing Dark Cloud over American Businesses." *In Business,* July/August, 1992.

a. Your company is going to start a WRAP program. Your business team must propose the best new pollution prevention idea. To get started, each member should gather information about pollution prevention methods currently employed by big corporations. You can find this kind of information by looking in various magazines and newspapers and by contacting local public environmental agencies.

b. Share your information with your business team members, and brainstorm to find a new pollution prevention method. Be sure to address the following points when presenting your proposal:
• Describe the method and how it will prevent pollution.
• Describe how the company will benefit from this method.

c. Present your proposal in a company meeting. When all the presentations have been made, the company will vote on the WRAP winner.

C. JARGON, BUZZWORDS, AND SLANG: POLLUTION-PREVENTION

Review these verb phrases from the reading. Then read the situations that follow and match each verb phrase with the situation that best illustrates its meaning:

a. to dump toxic waste   d. to increase recyclability
b. to reduce toxic waste   e. to accept liability
c. to cut toxic emissions   f. to enhance public image

1. __c__ Strict anti–air-pollution regulations mandated by the Clean Air Act should substantially reduce the release of hazardous chemicals into the atmosphere.

2. _____ A circuit board manufacturing company has modified its rinsing processes to separate the fluids that can be used further in rinsing and baths.

3. _____ Five beautiful cherry trees were planted at Bethseda–Chevy Chase High School through the efforts of Chevrolet/GEO and Evergreen, a local area volunteer tree-planting group.

4. _____ The largest of the nine sewage spills by the city of Los Angeles during the past seven years was 66 million gallons and occurred within a single day in 1992.

5. _____ Recent anti-pollution legislation could make environmental managers subject to criminal prosecution. Consequently, companies are moving more quickly to correct procedures that might violate such legislation.

6. _____ The EPA is trying to make the creation and disposal of toxic wastes so expensive that companies will adopt pollution prevention policies and programs.

D. PUTTING IT ALL TOGETHER

Study the following data from a survey conducted by The Kessler Exchange, a Northridge, California–based small-business research organization. With your business team, answer the following questions on a sheet of paper.

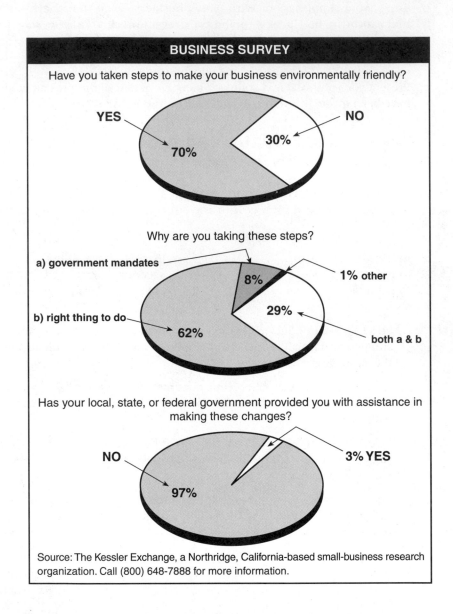

BUSINESS SURVEY

Have you taken steps to make your business environmentally friendly?

YES 70% **NO** 30%

Why are you taking these steps?

a) government mandates 8% 1% other

b) right thing to do 62% 29% both a & b

Has your local, state, or federal government provided you with assistance in making these changes?

NO 97% **3% YES**

Source: The Kessler Exchange, a Northridge, California-based small-business research organization. Call (800) 648-7888 for more information.

1. What do the pie charts tell you about the purpose of the survey?
2. What do you think response *b,* "right thing to do," means?
3. Since almost all of the respondents said that they receive no government assistance to make environmental changes, how do you think companies pay for these changes?

Gather information on the impact of environmental changes on local businesses by taking a trip to a local shopping center. Look for signs that show you which companies/stores/restaurants are attempting to be "environmentally responsible." Take notes on their products and practices. If possible, collect items such as brochures or sample products. Share your findings in a business team meeting. Discuss the impact the products and practices will have on both the environment and the participating businesses.

E. LISTENING FOR CORPORATE TIPS ON BECOMING ENVIRONMENTALLY FRIENDLY

You will hear a short talk about some of the pollution-prevention practices of two well-known companies. Listen for the following words. Make a check mark by each one you hear.

priority	unrecyclable	trademark
prime target	demonstrated	forerunner

IT WORKS!
Learning Strategy:
Listening for
Focus Words

[Now, listen to the speaker.]

Now, work with an associate to figure out the meanings of the focus words from the passage. Read the sentences and discuss the underlined words. Then write a brief definition for each underlined word.

> **EXAMPLE** John Paul Mitchell's company has made a <u>commitment</u> to the environment.
>
> commitment: _____*promise*_____

1. John Paul Mitchell made his commitment to the environment a <u>priority</u> from the start.

   priority: _____

2. Mr. Mitchell discourages employees from using disposable, often <u>unrecyclable</u>, containers.

   unrecyclable: _____

3. McDonald's <u>trademark</u> is their Golden Arches.

   trademark: _____

4. The disposability feature of McDonald's packaging became a <u>prime target</u> for protest.

   prime target: _____

5. Crowds of school children <u>demonstrated</u> outside several McDonald's restaurants.

   demonstrated: _____

6. Always a <u>forerunner</u> in the industry, McDonald's was quick to respond to protests over packaging.

   forerunner: _____

You will listen to the speaker again. Read the following questions. Listen for the information you'll need to answer them. Wait until you have finished listening before writing the answers on a sheet of paper.

1. What two things does Paul Mitchell insist on in the making of his products?
2. What does Mr. Mitchell expect of companies he does business with?
3. List two ways Mr. Mitchell rewards "environmentally responsible" employees.
4. What two things did the American public want that McDonald's delivered?
5. How did McDonald's respond to protests against its vast waste production?
6. List two steps McDonald's has taken to reduce waste.

[Listen again.]

F. PUTTING IT ALL TOGETHER: WHO ARE THE FORERUNNERS NOW?

Work with an associate. Find out about a company that is taking steps to improve its negative impact regarding a particular environmental concern.

NOTE In Business: The Magazine for Environmental Entrepreneuring, would be a good source of information for this activity.

Address the following points in your research:

• How has the company changed policies and/or products to lessen its negative impact on the environment?
• How has the company's image changed?
• How has this research influenced your opinion of this company?

G. ENVIRONMENTAL ISSUES AND CONSUMER BEHAVIOR

Following are results from a survey that rated the "environmental behavior" of adults, conducted by Cambridge Reports/Research International of Cambridge, Massachusetts, in July, 1991. With an associate, study the chart's survey results. Use the information to answer the questions and complete the activities that follow. Write your answers on a sheet of paper.

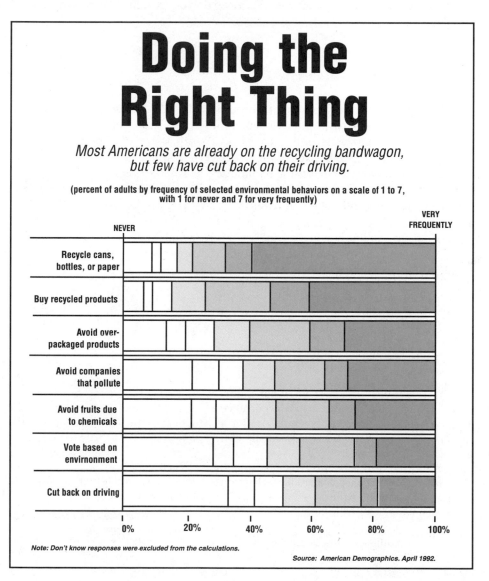

Doing the Right Thing

Most Americans are already on the recycling bandwagon, but few have cut back on their driving.

(percent of adults by frequency of selected environmental behaviors on a scale of 1 to 7, with 1 for never and 7 for very frequently)

Note: Don't know responses were excluded from the calculations.

Source: American Demographics. April 1992.

1. Write three conclusions you can make about what consumers will do to be environmentally responsible.
2. List the types of companies that can benefit from these conclusions, and give examples of the products they make.
3. Which "environmental behaviors" are more likely to be enforced by environmental laws rather than remain voluntary? Why?
4. What factors are most likely to determine what consumers *are* and what they *are not* willing to do to be environmentally responsible?

5. Conduct your own survey on consumer environmental behavior. Go to a public place where you can find many people—for example, a local market, shopping center, or library. Ask ten people to tell you, on a scale from 1 to 7, how willing they are to take steps to be environmentally responsible. To conduct your survey, use the seven questions from the Cambridge survey plus the following question: "Are you willing to pay more for products and services to be environmentally responsible? If so, approximately how much more?"

6. Record your survey results, and compare them with other associates' survey results in a business team meeting. How do your results compare to those of the Cambridge survey?

H. GREEN MARKETING

Companies are busy creating environmentally safe products and services to meet the demands of today's "environmentally responsible" consumer. Creating the product, however, is only part of it. To sell these environmentally safe products, companies must advertise effectively. You are going to read a short article about some new advertising techniques designed to get the attention of the environmentally conscious consumer. Before you read, write your answers to the following questions on a sheet of paper.

1. How do you know when a product is "environmentally safe"?
2. What kind of products have you bought that are "good" for the environment?
3. What do you think "green marketing" is?

Buying into the ads

by Laurel Pallock

There's a whole slew of new marketing techniques courting us consumers. Along with the old tried-and-true tricks of appealing to our vanity, our need to conform, or our respect for authority, here are a few of the latest ways we're parted from our disposable income:

Socially Conscious: Buy this T-shirt with its serious slogan and you'll make the world a better place and demonstrate how intelligent you are by your awareness.

Healthy Lifestyle: Get these running shoes and celebrate the unique you, someone who is physically healthy and wants to live in a health-conscious world.

Green Marketing: When nine out of ten consumers said in a national survey that they'd spend more for a product if it was environmentally safe, advertisers listened. Now, green marketing accounts for almost $50 billion in consumer product sales with its eco-buzz words:

Body Friendly
Nothing harsh or toxic here.

Water Friendly
We don't use phosphates, chlorine bleach or anything nondegradable.

Garbage Friendly
This is made from recycled, reusable, biodegradable ingredients and containers.

Air Friendly
Use this and you won't pollute anything or anyone or deplete the ozone layer.

Cruelty-Free
No animal was tested or harmed to bring this to your table.

Excerpted and adapted from "Buying into the Ads," by Laurel Pallock. San Francisco Chronicle, Aug. 11, 1992.

I. JARGON, BUZZWORDS, AND SLANG: GREEN MARKETING

The article lists five of the most popular "eco-buzz" words used to market environmentally safe products. With an associate, complete the table below by writing your own brief definition for each eco-buzz word and by describing a product, either real or imaginary, to match each term.

LEARNING STRATEGY

Remembering New Material: Writing your own definitions for new terms helps you remember them.

ECO-BUZZ WORD	DEFINITION	PRODUCT
Body Friendly	_____	_____
Water Friendly	_____	_____
Garbage Friendly	_____	_____
Air Friendly	_____	_____
Cruelty-Free	_____	_____

The following articles are about two businesses that offer unique alternatives to nonenvironmental products. Before you read them, take a moment to write your answers to these questions on a sheet of paper.

1. What is the most unusual environmental product you've seen on the market?
2. What are the most attractive features of this environmental product?
3. What features might cause you not to buy it?
4. What environmental product would you like to see on the market that you haven't seen yet?

Rubble with a cause

by Alessandra Bianchi

Architect Bob Noble envisions one day blanketing the globe with low-income housing made of recycled trash. After reading a graduate thesis on the subject, Noble licensed commercial-production rights to a molded structural material developed by the U.S. Department of Agriculture's Forest Products Laboratory, in Madison, Wis.

Called Gridcore, the product is made by mixing virtually any recycled materials—including wood, paper, cardboard, and some plastics—with hot water in a hydrapulper, "like a giant blender," says Noble. The blend is then screened, filtered, poured into a mold that suctions out the liquid, and heat-pressured into a ribbed structural panel. Two panels are then glued together to form a material that is competitively priced and up to "100 percent stronger than other structural panels of the same weight."

Noble launched his company, Gridcore Systems International, in April, 1992, with $1.5 million in private funds. He anticipates first-year revenues of $10 million. Initial demand has come from trade-show-display and entertainment industries, for which the product's light weight and low volume offer advantages in shipping, storage, and portability. Commercial introduction of Gridcore applications for larger structures is still two years away.

Excerpted and adapted from "Rubble with a Cause." Inc., July, 1993.

The grower of grease-eating bacteria

by Anita M. Samuels

For most people, fast food is as American as french fries. Unfortunately, over time, the oils used to prepare fast food can have the same clogging effects in drain pipes as they do in human arteries.

But for Bill Hadley, president of Environmental Biotech Inc., a Florida-based franchise network that grows bacteria, grease disposal is just a matter of unleashing microscopic bugs that consume and digest grease.

The process, known as bioremediation, breaks down the grease into carbon dioxide and water, which is much safer for the environment.

Dan Wimpy, a macrobiologist who works with the company, had identified more than a dozen natural bacterial strains that love to gorge on grease. Some prefer beef grease while others go for pork grease.

Mr. Hadley said the enzymes were injected into the drain lines and grease traps in kitchens. After the bacteria have done their jobs, other substances like disinfectant can kill them. The cleaning process costs about $220.

"The benefits to the customer are time and money because pipe blockage is very profitable to plumbers," said Mr. Hadley. Such a measure comes just in time to respond to a 1993 regulation by the Environmental Protection Agency, which prohibits the disposal of liquid waste into landfills.

Excerpted and adapted from "The Grower of Grease Eating Bacteria," by Anita M. Samuels. New York Times, October 25, 1992.

1. On a sheet of paper, write brief descriptions of both Gridcore and Bioremediation. Imagine that you are going to sell them to consumers. Address the following points in each description:
   • Explain how the product is made or how it works.
   • Use appropriate "eco-buzz" terms from Exercise I.
   • Compare traditional responsible alternatives to the product.
2. In a business team meeting, compare descriptions and come to a consensus on a description for both Gridcore and Bioremediation.
3. Conduct a survey with your business team. As you did in Exercise G, Item 5, find a place where you will find many people to survey. Half of your team will survey five "average consumers" on Gridcore, the other half on Bioremediation. First, you will have to briefly describe the product. Then ask the following questions:
   • Would you use this product?
   • Why or why not?
   • What type of environmental products do you usually buy?
   • What type of environmental products would you like to buy, but are not available?
4. Compile your business team's survey results. Provide the following information.
   a. Will products like Gridcore and Bioremediation be commonly used by the average consumer? Why or why not?
   b. Give examples of environmental products that are commonly used by average consumers.
   c. Make suggestions for the type of environmental products and/or services your business team would like to see on the market.

Evaluation

How well did you achieve the objectives for this chapter? List the results on a sheet of paper. Use the prompts that accompany each objective.

OBJECTIVES	RESULTS
Business	**Business**
1. To understand how environmental issues impact businesses	1. List two major changes a company might have to make to comply with environmental laws.
2. To research controversial environmental issues and to evaluate both sides of the debate	2. Give an example of "business vs. environmentalists," and briefly explain the arguments on both sides.
3. To learn about new methods and programs in business that focus on "environmental responsibility"	3. Describe an environmental corporate program or policy.
4. To analyze corporate motivation in taking steps to become more environmentally responsible	4. From a corporate point of view, state two advantages of being environmentally responsible.
5. To examine new products and business opportunities that respond to consumers' concern for the environment	5. Name two environmental products and explain why consumers would choose them over alternative products.
Language	**Language**
6. To practice negotiation and debate strategies	6. Write a statement that expresses why you think a particular environmental act should or should not be passed.
7. To express an argument using appropriate transition words and phrases	7. Write two statements, one that shows a relationship of contrast and one that shows a conclusion. Use the appropriate transition words.
8. To be able to use words and expressions related to the topic of environmental issues in business	8. Write two sentences that <u>each</u> contain words from this chapter relating to environmental issues in business.
Personal	**Personal**
_____	_____
_____	_____
_____	_____

Now, answer the following questions:

- What are your strengths in the area of environmental issues?
- How can you continue to learn about environmental issues in business on your own?

Startup Businesses: The Entrepreneurial Spirit

In this chapter you'll

- explore the motivations and attitudes of successful entrepreneurs.
- analyze difficulties facing entrepreneurs and learn how to overcome them.
- find out about different financing strategies for startup businesses.
- evaluate successful new products and services.
- review *wh*-clauses and practice using them.

> *Entrepreneurship is not an effect or a type of individual. It's a behavior. It's the pursuit of opportunity without regard to the resources you currently control.*
>
> —Howard S. Stevenson, professor of business at Harvard

An entrepreneur is someone who takes on a commercial enterprise with some degree of personal and financial risk. In this chapter, you will examine philosophies and practices that contribute to entrepreneurial success. You will evaluate the advantages of owning your own company and explore strategies to overcome the disadvantages. You will learn about creative methods of financing a startup company and research current startups. In the course of this chapter, you may also discover your own secret to entrepreneurial success.

PART I

Preparation

A. BRAINSTORMING

With a business team, look at the photos, discuss them, and on a sheet of paper, write your answers to the questions that follow.

1. Describe the entrepreneurs in the pictures. What type of people do you think they are?
2. What do you think motivated them to start their own companies?
3. How do their personalities and motivations help them to succeed?

B. WORKING WITH CONCEPTS: MOTIVATING FORCES

In the following article from *Entrepreneur* magazine, twelve contemporary, successful entrepreneurs answered the question, "What motivates you?" Before finding out what motivates them, look at the following list of adjectives. Circle the ones you think best describe a successful entrepreneur. If you think of other adjectives that describe an entrepreneur but are not listed, write them on a sheet of paper.

ethical	diplomatic	cautious	caring
sensitive	daring	organized	stubborn
educated	confident	greedy	outgoing
funny	patient	sincere	creative

Threads

Being in your business is working 80 hours a week so that you can avoid working 40 hours for someone else.

Ramona E. F. Arnett

Now, compare your list with an associate's. Explain to each other why you chose the adjectives you did. Then answer the following questions on a sheet of paper.

LEARNING STRATEGY

Personalizing: Sharing personal information helps you understand individual differences and improves your ability to communicate with many types of people.

1. Which adjectives best describe you?
2. Would you be a successful entrepreneur? Why or why not?
3. List three things that would motivate you to go into business for yourself (e.g., money, security).

Turn it on—motivational secrets from successful entrepreneurs

by Liza Leung

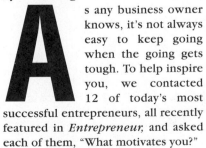

As any business owner knows, it's not always easy to keep going when the going gets tough. To help inspire you, we contacted 12 of today's most successful entrepreneurs, all recently featured in *Entrepreneur,* and asked each of them, "What motivates you?"

Kenneth Cole
Kenneth Cole Productions Inc.

"We appeal to the consumer in various ways—through wholesale, retail, footwear, leather goods, hosiery, legwear, and other related accessories. For me, the ability to relate to the consumer through all these vehicles is very inspiring, and doing business around the world makes it even more exciting and different."

Anita Roddick
The Body Shop Inc.

"Every time I walk by one of my shops and see what an educational role my company plays in a community, it sends chills down my spine, and I imagine that there couldn't ever be enough shops like these. In America, we have a shop in Harlem where 50 percent of the profits go into community development, and the other 50 percent go toward the funding of a similar shop elsewhere in the United States. The pride that shop brings to the staff and local residents motivates me.

"What The Body Shop does brilliantly is use our facilities in the street and shopping malls to talk about real human issues like AIDS, recycling, tribal rights, and community service or to encourage people to speak out against anything they perceive to be unjust. Knowing our products are emissaries of social change is really motivating."

Sheri Poe
Rykä Inc.

"Since I started this company in my kitchen seven years ago, I always dreamt of what it would be some day. Focusing on that vision helps me get through the tough times. Also, I think it's really important that the people you're working with are as committed to the same vision as you are, so you can support each other and keep each other motivated.

"Another thing that reenergizes me is when we introduce a product on the cutting edge that other manufacturers haven't done yet, and we receive a consumer's response like, 'Thank you. I've been looking for something like that.' That reenergizes me every time."

Howard Schultz
Starbucks Coffee Co.

"When everything matters, when you desire to consistently exceed expectations, when your motto is to 'underpromise and overdeliver,' you build a certain momentum that drives you forward. It is simply in my nature to reject mediocrity and raise the bar."

Frank Toskan
Make-Up Art Cosmetics (M.A.C.)

"One of the nicest things anyone ever said to me was, 'I hate makeup, but I love M.A.C.' That's what motivates me. Even people who don't wear makeup can appreciate our company, what it stands for, its philosophy, and the way we do business.

"We work from an inverted pyramid, where the customers are always at the top. Our customers inspire me and keep me going. They and our staff motivate me, not money. If I had stayed in this business just for the money, I would have de-motivated and closed down years ago."

Richard Melman
Lettuce Entertain You Enterprises

"A number of years ago, I was interviewed by someone who was writing a book on entrepreneurs. He asked me, 'What's the opposite of work?' I answered, 'Lazy.' He started laughing and said, 'Believe it or not, a lot of entrepreneurs say the same thing.' The average person thinks the opposite of work is play, but to an entrepreneur, work *is* play. I think it all adds up to having fun. When it stops being fun, I'll stop doing it."

Nicholas Graham
Joe Boxer Corp.

"Changing people's underwear is my duty in life—to change as many pairs of underwear as I can. It's a project that's never finished. There are always bigger and better ideas. When you get to one plateau, you've got to get to the next one."

Richard Foos, Harold Bronson
Rhino Records Inc.

Richard Foos: "Both Harold and I are passionate about the music we put out. In many ways, we put out the types of packages we as consumers would want."

Harold Branson: "Los Angeles inspires me—it's very stimulating and an extremely creative place. There's a lot of energy here, a sense that anything is possible, and that a lot of ideas, no matter how far-fetched, can be realized. This climate encourages you to be creative."

Jerry Greenfield and Ben Cohen
Ben & Jerry's Homemade Inc.

Jerry Greenfield: "I'm motivated by the people I work with. I'm very relationship-driven, which I think is different from most entrepreneurs. I'm inspired by doing things that are not normal and that most people think don't fit into the business world or don't make sense."

Ben Cohen: "Service to the community; creating something from nothing; discovering innovative ways of integrating concern for the community into daily business practice."

Jenny Craig
Jenny Craig International Inc.

"My motivation comes from our clients. I begin each business day by opening letters I've received from clients expressing their gratitude for the Jenny Craig Program. Each client relates a different life experience, but the common thread is how our program has improved the quality of their lives.

"With each letter, I realize that all the years [I've put] into developing an effective weight-management program have been worth the effort I have committed to this business. These letters, along with daily conversations with clients, keep me motivated to continue to provide the best program possible."

From "Turn It On—Motivational Secrets from Successful Entrepreneurs." Entrepreneur, May 1994.

C. JARGON, BUZZWORDS, AND SLANG: MOTIVATIONAL TALK

The following table will help you organize and focus on the motivational language in the passage you just read. The left column contains one phrase from each interview that helps answer the question, "What motivates you?" Follow these directions to complete the table:

- Use the middle column to write which entrepreneur/company the phrase comes from.
- Use the column on the right to write an additional phrase that expresses that entrepreneur's motivation.
- See the first entry as an example.

LEARNING STRATEGY

Managing Your Learning: Scanning a passage for specific details improves your reading skills.

MOTIVATION	ENTREPRENEUR/ COMPANY	ADDITIONAL MOTIVATION
Inverted pyramid: customer is always at the top	*Frank Toskan, M.A.C.*	*Belief in company philosophy*
Desire to exceed expectations		
Focusing on a vision		
Relating to the customer		
Social change		
Area/Place of business		
Doing things that don't fit into the business world		
Relating to clients' life experiences		
When it stops being fun, don't do it		
Bigger and better ideas		

D. PUTTING IT ALL TOGETHER

At the University of Houston's Small Business Development Center, researchers wanted to measure the influence of psychological and behavioral factors on getting into business. They asked 138 of the center's clients what motivated them to start their own businesses. You will find their answers to this question in the following survey results. Compare their answers to those of the twelve entrepreneurs you just read about.

BIGGEST MOTIVATION FOR STARTING A BUSINESS?	PERCENT OF CLIENTS WHO SAID THIS MOTIVATED THEM
Identified a market opportunity (i.e., had the right product at the right time)	37%
Wanted control and independence	32%
Wanted to make more money	9%
Wanted to make use of personal knowledge and experience	11%
Wanted to show they could do it	2%
Other (e.g., to learn, needed job, be creative, avoid taxes, God's will)	9%

Inc. magazine, July 1993, p. 47

In a business meeting, use the survey results and your completed table from Exercise C to help you discuss the following questions. Write your answers on a sheet of paper. Then do Activity 4.

1. The survey lists five main reasons entrepreneurs start their own businesses. Based on what the entrepreneurs you read about said, list four additional factors that motivate people to start a company.
2. What types of motivation do you think are most important to an entrepreneur's success? (e.g., the desire to be creative, to make money, to have fun.)
3. Now that you have learned about what motivates entrepreneurs, list six adjectives that come to your mind when you think of the word "entrepreneur."
4. Individually research a successful entrepreneur. Good sources for this are business magazines and books on entrepreneurs in your library. Usually, profiles about successful entrepreneurs tell interesting stories about how they became successful. Use the following guidelines to help you organize your research:
   - Who is the entrepreneur?
   - What product or service does his or her company provide?
   - What interesting story can you tell about this person that shows the type of person he or she is?
   - What seems to motivate this person?

Communication Memo • Communication Memo • Communication Memo

TO: All Employees
FROM: Corporate Communications Department
RE: Combining sentences using *wh*-clauses

To help you write about entrepreneurs, read this corporate review on combining sentences using *wh*-clauses.

If you use *wh*-clauses to tell a story, you can add important and interesting details without interfering with the main idea. Using *wh*-clauses to combine sentences makes your spoken and written English smoother and livelier:

Fred Smith was so down on his luck at one point that he told H. H. McAdams, <u>***wh*o was suing him for a $2 million fraudulent loan**</u>, that he was going to kill himself by jumping out the window.

In the sentence:

- The main point is that Fred Smith told H. H. McAdams that he was going to jump out of the window.
- The *wh*-clause follows and describes H. H. McAdams, the preceding important detail.
- Since H. H. McAdams is a person, 'who' is used to introduce the *wh*-clause.
- The *wh*-clause is embedded in the sentence that expresses the main point.

To further understand how this structure is formed, read the following two sentences:

<u>Main idea sentence:</u>
Smith left Yale University to take over his family's small airline brokering business.

<u>Important/interesting detail sentence:</u>
Smith originally thought of the idea for Federal Express at Yale University.

Now read this sentence that combines them:

Smith left Yale University, <u>***wh*ere he originally thought of the idea for Federal Express**</u>, to take over his family's small airline brokering business.

Enc.
CM/ja

Memo Attachment

Read the following pairs of sentences. Then embed the "detail" sentence into the "main idea" sentence by using a *wh*-clause that begins with the *wh*-word given for each pair. Write the combination sentence for each pair on a sheet of paper.

Here's an example:

- *Where:*

Main idea sentence:
Fred's idea was that small planes would bring the packages to a central location, and then jetliners would deliver them anywhere in the world.

Detail sentence:
At this location, night workers would unload, sort, and reload packages onto different planes.

Combination sentence:
Fred's idea was to have all the packages come to a central location, _**wh**ere night workers would unload, sort, and reload packages_, and then jetliners would deliver them anywhere in the world.

1. *Which:*
   Main idea:
   In 1971, Smith promised stock in his family's company to obtain the $2 million loan.
   Detail:
   The company never approved the promise.

2. *Where:*
   Main idea:
   Smith went to Las Vegas and made $27,000 at the blackjack tables.
   Detail:
   Smith gambled the last few hundred dollars he had.

3. *Who:*
   Main idea:
   In 1974, unhappy investors stripped Smith of control and made General "Howling" Estes the company's new president.
   Detail:
   General Howling ran the commercial charter line, World Airways.

4. *When:*
   Main idea:
   In 1975 he was reinstated as CEO.
   Detail:
   In 1975, he was found "not guilty" on criminal fraud charges.

LEARNING STRATEGY

Remembering New Material: Retelling a story helps you remember the interesting details.

E. DEBRIEFING

Share your "successful entrepreneur" story from Exercise D with your business team members. Be prepared to answer the four questions in Item 3 and to include additional details you found interesting.

F. SETTING OBJECTIVES

Following are the goals for this chapter. Read them, and consider your personal goals for this chapter. At the end of this chapter, on page 166, you'll list your results.

OBJECTIVES

Business
1. To explore the motivations and attitudes of successful entrepreneurs
2. To learn about different kinds of entrepreneurs and how they became successful
3. To understand obstacles facing entrepreneurs and learn strategies to overcome them
4. To find out about new products and services and predict whether or not they will be successful
5. To learn how entrepreneurs use creative financing strategies to get their businesses started

Language
6. To understand and be able to use words and expressions related to the topic of entrepreneurs
7. To review *wh*-clauses and practice using them
8. To improve your English language skills through role-playing and outside research

Personal

_____

_____

_____

Integration

A. HARDSHIPS AND REWARDS

Threads

Academic Systems, Inc., a Palo Alto, California-based start-up, is testing software that can assess students' strengths and weaknesses and tailor college courses to their specific needs.

San Francisco Chronicle
11/22/94

Behind most entrepreneurial successes are stories of overcoming obstacles and defying conventional wisdom. The following passage was written by an entrepreneur who has challenged tradition and endured hardships. Before you read, discuss your answers to these questions with a business team.

1. List three obstacles minority entrepreneurs like the woman in the photo are likely to face in their careers as business owners.
2. What is "conventional wisdom?" What kind of conventional wisdom might minority entrepreneurs have to defy to reach their goals?
3. Imagine being your own boss. What would you like about it? What wouldn't you like?

El 'querer es poder'—if you want something badly enough, you can get it

by Isabel Medina

After three years at New York University, I left, at the time, to take a six-month break and come back the next semester. I needed time to sort things out. Not having a family that had been college educated made it tough to make some decisions. This was my first exposure to having to make decisions by myself that would affect the rest of my life.

I left school and got a job in an import-export company. I had no office skills but soon realized how invaluable my speaking, reading, and writing Spanish was. I recall, as a child, how I rebelled when Mom insisted that we all sit at the kitchen table for an hour as she tutored us in Spanish. I hated it then because all the other children were out playing and here I was studying again after a full school day. I later appreciated the time taken out for these lessons. Mom's idea was that we had to learn English in school but that we would never forget our Hispanic roots, culture, or language.

I had my greatest success when I owned a metal fabrication factory. We did machining, welding, and brazing there. I was in a nontraditional field for a woman, and I did receive some flack. However, behaving like a lady—but one that knew what she was talking about—won me many friends in this arena. After proving myself, competitively, price-wise, and quality-wise, I was treated as one of the "boys." At this point in my business life I negotiated one of the biggest contracts of my life. I won the bid competitively from the government, was the low bidder, and then was rejected. I learned to put my fighting gloves on then. I called my attorney, fought for the contract, and won. At this same time I was elected as a delegate to the White House Conference on Small Business.

This was my training ground for getting involved on a national level for Hispanics and women business owners. At the time that I completed this major contract I realized that these jobs were drying up. Large corporations were bidding for the same jobs I was, and I could not compete price-wise against them. Lessons learned: When you realize that the money and contracts are not coming in, cut back on everything; cut your losses and look for new sources of revenue. Never be afraid to be creative.

In 1986 I was again elected to the White House Conference on Small Business. Again, it was a wonderful learning experience. There were also disappointments. One of the greatest was the support of the delegates across the nation for the "English Only" bill. We should realize that as the world gets smaller, learning foreign languages will become a crucial business tool. How can we talk about international sales unless we learn the languages and cultures of the world that surrounds us?

I have been in all different fields of business. I have been in manufacturing, foods, and promotional items, yet I have found them all to be essentially the same. Owning your own business means that you work without looking at a time clock. It means that you learn to market your company and/or its products or skills, to talk to your accountant intelligently, and to read your own P & L (Profit and Loss) statements. You find out that although your employees get paid every week, you may not get a paycheck. All these lessons just mean that as a business owner, you work harder, longer, perhaps get paid less, and only you can pat yourself on the back when something goes very well. It is primarily learning to believe in yourself, and doing what you have to do.

As individuals we are made up of many different layers. I have used my education, my culture, my ethnicity, and my femininity to enhance my walk through the business world. I have never forgotten that whatever I take out I must replenish. My weaknesses became my strengths, and that is how I look at the business world; a great challenge, and always new horizons to explore and many mountains to climb. But, I have never forgotten to give back to my community, or to my fellow business people.

Excerpted from "El 'Querer es Poder'— If You Want Something Badly Enough You Can Get It." From The Woman Entrepreneur: 33 stories of personal success. Upstart Publishing Company, Inc. 1992. pp. 99-104.

B. ANALYZING WHAT YOU'VE READ

Working with an associate, discuss the following questions about the passage you just read. Write the answers on a sheet of paper.

1. Describe the characteristics and attitudes that have helped Isabel Medina become a successful entrepreneur.
2. What do you think Ms. Medina means by "My weaknesses became my strengths"?
3. Ms. Medina devotes a paragraph to her "greatest success." Describe what you think was her greatest achievement during that time.
4. Ms. Medina says she "received some flack" when she started her metal fabrication factory. Who do you think gave her "flack," and how did they probably behave around her?
5. Even though Ms. Medina was the low bidder for the government contracts, she was rejected. Why do you think that happened?
6. Explain what Ms. Medina means when she advises, "Never be afraid to be creative."
7. How do foreign languages become "business tools" as the "world gets smaller"?

C. JARGON, BUZZWORDS, AND SLANG: BUSINESS OWNERSHIP

Write the letter of the word or phrase on the line next to its definition.

a. flack
b. low bidder
c. business tool
d. to dry up
e. to cut your losses

_____ to abandon an unprofitable venture before the losses become too great

_____ ridicule or giving someone a difficult time

_____ to stop producing or become unprofitable

_____ something that facilitates success in business

_____ a person offering a service at a price that is lower than the prices of other businesses competing to perform the same service

Now check your understanding of the words and phrases from the passage by paraphrasing the sentence in which they appear. Write your sentences on a sheet of paper, replacing the underlined word or phrase without changing the meaning of the sentence.

EXAMPLE I had no office skills but soon realized how <u>invaluable</u> my speaking, reading, and writing Spanish was.
Paraphrase: Even though I didn't have office skills, I soon found out that my ability to speak, read and write Spanish was <u>extremely important</u> in business.

1. I was in a nontraditional field for a woman, and I did receive some <u>flack</u>.
2. I was the <u>low bidder</u> and then was rejected.
3. I realize that the government contract jobs were <u>drying up</u>.
4. When the money stops coming in, you have to <u>cut your losses</u> and look for new sources of revenue.
5. As the world gets smaller, learning foreign languages will become an <u>essential business tool.</u>

D. PUTTING IT ALL TOGETHER

In a business team, read and imagine the following situations. Then choose one of the situations to act out with your business team. Discuss the situation, assign roles, and prepare for a performance in a company meeting. Do your best to put yourself "in the shoes" of the person you are going to play in these emotionally charged situations.

Understanding and Using Emotions: Analyzing emotions in a hypothetical situation helps you express your own emotions in a real situation.

1. Isabel Medina is on site at her metal fabrication company. She's having a meeting with two or three male supervisors regarding the level of product quality she expects them to monitor on the production lines. She emphasizes the seriousness of this issue with regards to the government contracts she'll be bidding for. The men are skeptical of her knowledge and seem to be resisting her authority. This can be determined by their comments, questions, tone, and body language. In other words, they are giving her "flack."

2. Isabel is in a meeting with government building contractors discussing a contract to build a new post office she has recently bid on. She knows she was the low bidder, yet the contractors reject her offer. She realizes she has to "put her fighting gloves on" if she's going to win the contract. The discussion involves the pricing and quality of Isabel's products and the government contractors' method of choosing who gets the contract.

3. Isabel is at a White House Conference on Small Business. She is debating the "English Only" bill with two or three other delegates. If Congress passes the bill, English will become the official language of the United States under federal law. The arguments for and against the bill are based on how the bill will affect international business as the world becomes smaller.

During the role-plays, take a moment to evaluate the appropriateness of the "actors" in one of the situations. Check whether you think the participants' level of formality, tone of voice, and nonverbal behavior were appropriate or inappropriate. Also write brief comments or suggestions.

FEATURE	APPROPRIATE	INAPPROPRIATE	COMMENTS AND SUGGESTIONS
Level of Formality			
Tone			
Nonverbal behavior			

E. LISTENING: INTERVIEW WITH AN ENTREPRENEURIAL FAMILY

You are going to hear a news story about the McGregors, a family of entrepreneurs, who have overcome very difficult times before seeing their dream become a reality.

Before you listen, discuss the questions with an associate. Write your answers on a sheet of paper.

IT WORKS!
Learning Strategy:
Thinking About
a Topic Before
You Listen
for Information
About It

- What specific difficulties do you think this family overcame?
- Of all the things you have, e.g., possessions, free time, etc., what would you be willing to sacrifice to get your company off the ground?
- How can overcoming difficulties help or hinder entrepreneurs' future success?

Read the following questions and listen for the information to answer them. Wait until you've finished listening, then write your answers on a sheet of paper. Compare your answers with those of an associate.

1. What is the McGregors' latest invention?
2. What are this product's advantages?
3. What is the McGregors' company's name?
4. What makes their success story so extraordinary?
5. Just when things were at their worst, what happened?
6. What new developments are happening in their company?

[Now, listen to the news report.]

Before you listen again, read the following questions. To answer them, you'll need to listen for details and make deductions about what you've heard. When you've finishing listening, discuss the questions with an associate. Write your answers on a sheet of paper.

Threads

Vision is the art of seeing things invisible.

Jonathan Swift

1. How does the McGregors' lastest invention differ from similar products on the market?
2. "Dad" McGregor is called the "visionary." What do you think that means?
3. When referring to the McGregors' experiences, the newscaster says, "the scars run deep." Explain what she means by that.
4. How do you think the McGregors' past experiences affect their business decisions and daily lives today?

[Listen again to the news report.]

F. PUTTING IT ALL TOGETHER

At the time of the McGregors' interview, their company was about to be involved in an "IPO." To increase your knowledge of entrepreneurs and startup companies, conduct the following research:

Threads

IPOs raised $41.5 billion in 1992, up 72% from 1992, which was also a record year.

Investment Dealers Digest, 1994

1. Find out what an IPO is.
2. Gather information on three companies currently involved in IPOs. This information can be found in the business sections of most major newspapers.
3. Decide which of the IPOs you would choose to be involved in if you could.
4. Share your findings in a business team meeting.

G. FINANCE TACTICS: BOOTSTRAPPING

Starting a business is always a financial risk; consequently, finding ways to finance a new venture is usually a challenge. In the following passage, you will read about how some entrepreneurs were able to get their companies off the ground with some clever "bootstrapping," that is, with little or none of their own money. Before you read, discuss the following questions with an associate and write your answers on a sheet of paper.

- If you had a great idea for a new business, how would you begin to find financing for it?
- If you were unable to get money to back your idea, what could you do to at least get the product made *without* any money?
- What do you think "bootstrapping" is?

The secrets of bootstrapping

by Robert A. Mamis

In the last decade many businesses that began with absolutely no capital have grown more briskly than businesses that were awash in it. Their brilliance has come through figuring out how to tap the money of others, or how to substitute imagination, knowledge, or sweat for money in the first place. That's all bootstrapping is.

The bootstrapping founders in these pages tend not to have had vast empires in mind when they started companies. They had the less risky goal of securing a modest corner of entrepreneurial turf. Unlike the more daring, niche-exploiting entrepreneurs of the 80s, today's entrepreneurs are likely to be miroexploiters within a niche: offering a fresh twist on how someone else is doing something, a product that another has neglected to deliver, or a service that others don't provide. No doubt, the "American Dream" has shrunk to the 90's tough economic environment.

At this time, there's no course book of bootstrapping techniques, but there ought to be. As the following advice demonstrates, the approach has much to teach.

1. *Get in on the dawn of an era.* New niches pop up with regularity these days, but they don't come with ready-made standards for how to conduct business. Those practices develop over time, and until they do, bootstrappers have unique opportunities. When the "900" pay-per-minute phone service was introduced in the late 80s, a flood of merchants entered the market at the other end of the line. It occurred to only a handful, among them Worthington Voice Services, Inc., of Worthington, Ohio, to develop and market computerized systems to handle the incoming calls. Founders Gregory Speicher and De Trinh dropped out of jobs in the PC industry, pooled $800 to buy an accessory that allowed them to digitize speech, programmed the software, and constructed a demo. Working out of Speicher's mother's basement, the two cold-called "900-number" companies to sell them on their idea. When they got orders, they asked for up-front deposits to cover the purchase of the hardware—virtually the *entire* cost.

2. *Tap vendors.* This "put-it-to-'em" tactic works best in economically tough times, when vendors and suppliers can be persuaded to extend credit even to the uncreditworthy. Like many bootstrappers, cofounder of ABL Electronics Corp., in Timonium, Maryland, tried to get his suppliers to extend long credit terms even as he was persuading his customers to pay invoices promptly. "We expected COD from our customers, but we *paid* net 45 or net 60," he admits. "I don't see anything wrong with using your vendors to help fund your business."

3. *Establish in locales with lots of vacancies.* Almost any bootstrapped enterprise can carve out a favorable deal in areas where landlords are desperate for the slightest promise of tenancy. Around 1986, Houston was such a setting. Forest Henson, Jr., who founded JTS Enterprises, Inc., in 1986, struck up an arrangement with a Houston landlord for a three-year lease that called for virtually no rent early on. "The landlord gambled that we'd *both* last three years," he remembers fondly. Lesson learned: Act fast if a prime location is available cheap.

4. *Don't sell at retail when you can take orders at wholesale.* Stuck (by choice) in the sparsely populated reaches of central Maine, with no phone and electricity, Roxanne Quimby and her partner, Burt Shavitz, started a business they called Burt's Bees. Quimby and Shavitz bottled honey in kitchen canning jars, cast candles out of beeswax on a wood stove, loaded the finished lot into a pickup truck, and drove off to sell their goods at crafts fairs. After two years, it struck Quimby that, "being on the road every weekend and coming back and making candles and going on the road again was ridiculous." Plus, their market was limited to the territories their tired old Datsun could cover. So they pooled their meager resources and rented space at a *wholesale* show. That, Quimby says, is when business took off. "We concentrated totally on wholesale," she says, "because it was easier to open markets." The company now sells more than 100 gift and skin-care products and is about to launch a line of clothing. In 1992, it took in around $4.2 million.

5. *Fake it till you make it.* Being new and tiny, how do bootstrappers assure suppliers and customers of their ability to pay or deliver? By convincing them they're *not* new and tiny. "One thing I realized very quickly is that people want to see fancy offices, fancy letterhead, fancy everything," says founder Michael Kempner of MWW/Strategic Communications Inc., in Rivers Edge, N.J. He didn't have fancy anything, but he had a friend in advertising who did. Kempner moved into the friend's office at no expense, with the understanding that his public relations firm would steer advertising in his friend's direction. He even moved in on the ad company's name, MWW: I put a slash behind MWW, and added, 'Strategic Communications,' and it looked like I was part of a big company. It was all a mirage at the beginning. As far as my clients knew, here I was with a fancy name in a fancy office, with forty people working for me. I never told clients those people *didn't* work for me, and they never asked. Since then, the ad company, MWW, has gone under, but Kempner's company is flourishing. "Now that the company's not fake anymore, I'd like to change the name," says Kempner, "I hate it, but it's too late."

6. *Get several bank loans.* If borrowing from a bank seems improbable to a bootstrapper, think how borrowing from *four* institutions must seem. Says Barry Mower of American Playworld: "We needed about $16,000. I applied for four different loans at once— short-term loans such as those from credit unions—on the basis of my personal credit. I had to apply simultaneously in order to do it; otherwise, the applications would have counted against one another. The interest was four times what it should have been, but this was desperation financing."

7. *Perform cheap market research.* Undecided whether to quit their salaried jobs and go into business, Randy Amon and his partner, of ABL Electronics, implemented what they recall fondly as, "the market-research minute": they called up one computer store. "We asked them, 'If we made a cable that connected opposing equipment, would you buy it?'" Amon relates. "Not only would they buy it, they placed an order with us on the phone. We didn't even have a company yet, or a product. They said they'd pay us $35 apiece for five cables. We went out and bought the stuff to make them with—$60 from my pocket and $40 from my partner's." To this day, that ratio remains the split of business ownership.

Excerpted and adapted from "The Secrets of Bootstrapping." Inc., September, 1992. pp. 71–84.

H. ANALYZING WHAT YOU'VE READ

To get a better understanding of the bootstrapping methods you've read about, review the passage and create an outline that captures the main points and important details of each bootstrapping method. Use a style of outlining that works most effectively for you. Following are three different outlining styles; use one of them, or one of your own.

LEARNING STRATEGY

Managing Your Learning: Trying new ways to organize material helps you find which way works best for you.

Style #1:

I. Dawn of an Era
    A. Find a "niche" product:
        1. fills an important need
        2. not much competition
        3. "newness" will attract orders
    B. Example:
        1. "900-number" accessory
            a. computerized
            b. handles incoming calls
        2. Worthington Voice Services Inc., Ohio
            a. two guys—left PC industry
            b. cold-called from basement
            c. up-front deposits
II. etc.

Style #2:

METHOD	EXAMPLE OF A PRODUCT	EXAMPLE OF A COMPANY
Dawn of an Era: Find "niche" —fills need —little competition —"newness" attracts orders	"900-number" accessory: —computerized —handles incoming calls	Worthington Voice Svcs., Ohio: —two ex-PC guys —cold-called from basement —up-front deposits

Style #3:

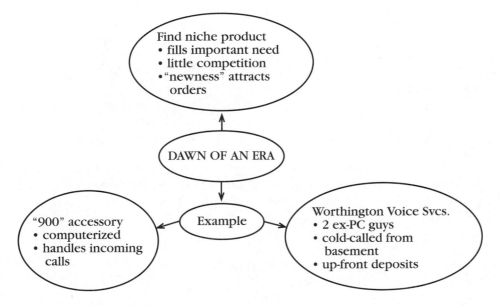

Your Style: On a sheet of paper, create your own outline for each of the remaining bootstrapping methods.

I. JARGON, BUZZWORDS, AND SLANG: BOOTSTRAPPING TALK

With an associate, discuss the definitions you are given for each of the following verb phrases from the article. Decide which is the best definition for each verb phrase.

to find a new niche	to launch a new product
to pay net 45	to wholesale
to perform market research	to cold-call

To find a new niche is to
  a. have a product that is better than your competitors'.
  b. discover a need for a new product or service.
  c. test a new product.

To launch a new product is to
  a. start selling a product that your company hasn't sold before.
  b. sell a new product in foreign markets.
  c. discontinue existing products in order to sell a new product.

To pay net 45 is to
  a. pay 45% of a bill.
  b. put all your bills together and pay them every 45 days.
  c. have 45 days to pay a bill.

To wholesale is to
  a. sell directly to consumers.
  b. sell whole units, not parts or accessories.
  c. sell in large quantity and lower the price per unit.

To perform market research is to
  a. shop for products that compete with your product.
  b. predict your product's success by studying what consumers want.
  c. give away samples of your product.

To cold-call is to
  a. call back potential customers after they say "no" the first time.
  b. call potential customers during non–business hours.
  c. call potential customers the first time with no prior introduction.

Use the verb phrases from the preceding list to complete the sentences. Then, to check your understanding of the terms, answer the questions that follow on a sheet of paper using information from the article and your own ideas.

1. Without having to deal with the ready-made standards of conducting an established business, bootstrappers can take advantage of unique opportunities if they _find a new niche_____ .
   • What are two examples of a new niche product?

2. In tough economic times, vendors will often allow even the "uncreditworthy"

   to _____ .
   • In what ways does this method help the bootstrapper?

3. A good way to get feedback on whether your new product is as good as you

   think it is is to _____ .
   • Give two examples of performing this method as cheaply as possible.

4. To build a customer base, without any existing customer contacts,

   bootstrappers often have to _____ .
   • Give two positive aspects of this sales method and two negative aspects.

5. Although retail brings in more profit per item, sometimes it's wiser to

   _____ .
   • What are the advantages of this method over retail?

6. To keep existing customers interested, as well as attract new customers, a

   successful company will periodically _____ .
   • If you were a business owner, what factors would you consider before employing this method to expand your business?

J. PUTTING IT ALL TOGETHER

You have learned about several methods to get a business started with little or no money. Still, these are only a few of the many ways entrepreneurs get financing for their ventures.

To broaden your knowledge of how to finance a new business, find a public organization, such the Small Business Association (SBA), or a local entrepreneurs group. Go to the office or to a meeting in person. Gather as much information as you can on financing startup companies: ask questions, collect data, listen to and participate in conversations. Later, outline the main points and important details on paper so you can share what you learn with your associates.

Evaluation

How well did you achieve the objectives for this chapter? List your results on a sheet of paper. Use the prompts that accompany each objective.

OBJECTIVES	RESULTS
Business	**Business**
1. To explore the motivations and attitudes of successful entrepreneurs	1. Give three examples of what motivates entrepreneurs to succeed.
2. To learn about different kinds of entrepreneurs and how they became successful	2. Briefly describe how two entrepreneurs employed different methods to find success.
3. To understand obstacles facing entrepreneurs and learn strategies to overcome them	3. Name two common obstacles in starting up a company, and give examples of how to overcome them.
4. To find out about new products and services and predict whether or not they will be successful	4. Describe a new product from a startup company and explain why you think it will be successful.
5. To learn how entrepreneurs use creative financing to get their businesses started	5. Briefly explain two methods that entrepreneurs use to finance a startup company.
Language	**Language**
6. To understand and be able to use words and expressions related to the topic of entrepreneurs	6. Write two sentences that each contain a word or phrase related to the topic of entrepreneurs.
7. To review *wh*-clauses and practice using them	7. Write two sentences that each contain an embedded *wh*-clause.
8. To improve your English language skills through role-playing and outside research	8. Briefly describe how either role-playing or an outside experience related to this chapter has changed your English.
Personal	**Personal**
_____	_____
_____	_____
_____	_____

Now, answer the following questions:

- What are your strengths in the area of entrepreneurs and startup companies?
- How can you continue to learn about entrepreneurs and startup companies on your own?

Global Economics and You

CHAPTER PREVIEW

In this chapter you'll

- learn about basic economic indicators.
- analyze the impact of changing economies on international business.
- learn about international trade policies and trade agreements.
- practice your English by discussing the global economy outside of class.
- discover how global economics affects you and your future.

> *It is probably not love that makes the world go round, but rather those mutually supportive alliances through which partners recognize their dependence on each other in the achievement of shared and private goals..*

—Fred Allen, chairman, Pitney Bowes Company, 1979

This chapter focuses on how the nations of the world are economically interrelated through trade and how our lives are affected by economic policies. You will analyze how changing economies impact businesses around the world. You will explore the history of global trade agreements and evaluate current trade negotiations. You will also be able to discuss current economic issues in international business.

PART I

Preparation

A. BRAINSTORMING

In a meeting with your associates, look at the photo and discuss the following questions. Write your answers on a sheet of paper.

- Where do you think this scene takes place?
- List the products that you think are manufactured in that country and which are probably imported from other countries.
- How would you describe the standard of living in this place? Why?

Forming Concepts: Discussing pictures helps you brainstorm about a new topic and remember information.

B. WORKING WITH CONCEPTS: ECONOMIC INDICATORS

Read the following article from *The Economist,* dated November 16, 1991. Before you read it, discuss these questions with an associate and write your answers on a sheet of paper.

- Economists study increases and decreases in certain areas, such as unemployment, to determine the economic strength of a country. What are some other areas that they probably study?
- List four factors of everyday life that indicate a "healthy" economy.

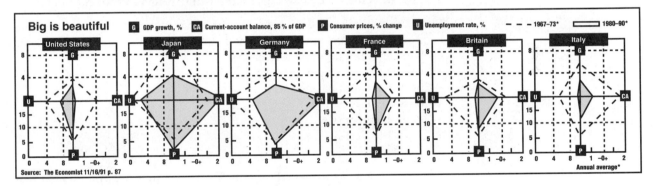

An economy's best friend

from *The Economist*

Traditionally, governments have had four main economic goals: strong growth, low inflation, low unemployment, and a "sound" balance-of-payments position. One rough-and-ready way to judge how an economy measures up to these goals is the "diamond," invented by economists at the Organization for Economic Cooperation and Development (OECD), the Paris-based club of rich nations, in the early 1980s.

The charts plot each of the four economic indicators (GDP growth, inflation, unemployment rate, and current-account balance) along one of the four axes, with the scales fixed so that the farther each plot is away from the origin, the better the country's performance. For each, the four plots are joined up to form a diamond: the bigger the diamond, the better its record.

The charts compare the performance of the six biggest industrial economies in 1980–90 with the "golden age" of 1967–73, before oil prices soared. In the 1960s and early 1970s most economies scored relatively well on all four criteria. Japan and Germany boasted the biggest diamonds, but then came the oil shock: growth stalled, inflation and unemployment rose. All countries saw their diamonds shrink dramatically during 1974–79, particularly Britain and Italy.

During the 1980s, unemployment continued to rise everywhere, and economic growth was slower in all countries than it had been between 1967–73. America's diamond got smaller in all areas because of its huge account-balance deficit.

The charts show that only two of these countries regained their sparkle during the 1980s. Only Japan and Germany lowered their inflation records of 1967–73 and managed current-account surpluses. Their diamonds puffed up almost to the size they had been before the oil shock.

Excerpted and adapted from "An Economy's Best Friend." The Economist, November 16, 1991. p. 87

C. JARGON, BUZZWORDS, AND SLANG: ECONOMICS TALK

1. The article talks about four economic indicators:
   • GDP growth (G)
   • current-account balance (CA)
   • consumer prices (P)
   • unemployment rate (U)

   Match the letter for each indicator with the appropriate definition.

   _____ **a.** Percentage of people in a country who are not working

   _____ **b.** Gross Domestic Product: the total increase in value of goods produced and services provided in a country in one year

   _____ **c.** Ratio between the revenue a country generates from the goods and services it exports and the amount it spends on the goods and services it imports

   _____ **d.** Percentage of average increase in consumer product prices

2. Read the following article excerpts that give information about the four economic indicators you have learned about. Work with an associate. Read each excerpt and decide if it refers to:
   • Gross Domestic Product (GDP)
   • Current-Account Balance (CA)
   • Consumer Prices (P)
   • Unemployment (U)

   EXAMPLE

   GDP
   _____ "Economists for Merrill Lynch & Co. said they are encouraged that new orders for computers and communications equipment, possibly a better indicator of manufacturing growth, rebounded in February after a January drop." (*San Francisco Chronicle,* March 31, 1994)

   _____ **a.** "In response to U.S. demands for a reduction of the trade deficit, Japan announced deregulation measures for nine industries, from construction to insurance, opening them to foreign competition." (*Los Angeles Times,* March 30, 1994)

   _____ **b.** "Big gains at U.S. aircraft manufacturers pushed factory orders up a healthy 2.1% in January from December. Orders for aircraft and aircraft parts pushed transportation orders up 14% to $41 billion." (*USA Today,* March 4, 1994)

   _____ **c.** "The evidence suggests that immigrants create at least as many jobs as they take, and that their presence should not be feared by U.S. workers." (*San Francisco Chronicle,* March 22, 1994)

   _____ **d.** "The 20% nationwide inflation was caused in part by an excess money supply typical of the Lunar New Year holiday, which was in February. China also eased credit late last year to aid state enterprises and to cover salary increases for civil servants." (*Wall Street Journal,* March 23, 1994)

D. PUTTING IT ALL TOGETHER

Discuss the following questions with an associate. Some of the answers you will find in the text. For others, you will need to rely on your ability to deduce—draw logical conclusions—from the information you are given. Write your answers on a sheet of paper.

LEARNING STRATEGY

Overcoming Limitations: Applying abstract information to specific examples improves your understanding.

1. What are the four main economic goals of a government?
2. The article states that a worldwide oil shortage—the "oil shock"—caused inflation and unemployment to rise. What type of products do you think rose in price? What type of jobs were lost?
3. Imagine there were an oil shortage now. Describe how your daily life would change if oil was suddenly very difficult to get and very expensive if you could get it.
4. The article states that from 1980 to 1990 Japan and Germany had current-account surpluses; that is, they exported more than they imported. What types of products do you think these countries exported?
5. Think about yourself. List some products that you have bought that were made in these countries: United States; Japan; Germany; France; Britain; Italy.
6. The charts in the article indicate that from 1980 to 1990, the United States, France, Britain, and Italy had an account-balance deficit; they imported more than they exported. At the same time, unemployment was quickly rising. What industries in these countries probably lost the most jobs? Think about your answers to Items 3 and 5 to help you answer this question.
7. What industries have you considered for your own future employment? In what country are you planning to pursue your career?
8. The global economy affects everyone. The following activity will illustrate how the global economy can potentially affect your future career. On your own, research a country and an industry you have considered for future employment. The following texts will help you gather the information necessary to do this. You can find them in the reference section at your school or public library.
   • Foreign Economic Trends
   • World Economic Index
   • U.N. Import/Export information
   • World Book Encyclopedia

IT WORKS!
Learning Strategy:
Relating a New
Topic to a
Personal Situation

Fill out the following Career Forecast form to complete your research:

CAREER FORECAST

1. Future industry/profession: _____
   _____

2. Future country of employment: _____
   _____

3. Why are you considering this industry/profession? _____
   _____

4. In this country, has inflation increased or decreased in the last year? _____
   _____

5. In this country, has unemployment increased or decreased in the last year? _____
   _____

6. Does this country have an account-balance surplus or deficit? _____
   _____

7. In what industries has the most employment and unemployment occurred? _____
   _____

8. Which industries are growing, and which are declining? _____
   _____

9. What type of product or service will you be providing? _____
   _____

10. Is this product exported? If so, to what countries? _____
    _____

11. In your opinion, will your industry grow, decline, or stay the same in the next five to ten years?
    Explain your answer. _____
    _____

12. How has this research changed your feelings and/or your approach toward your career goals? (For example, is the industry likely to provide long-term employment? Does this industry rely heavily on other countries, and if so, would learning another language increase your career advancement?) _____
    _____
    _____
    _____

E. DEBRIEFING MEETING

In a business team, share your information about the country and industry you researched. Identify any products that are probably traded among the countries your team researched. Discuss your answer to Question 12 on the Career Forecast form, and offer comments and suggestions about your associates' career goals.

F. SETTING OBJECTIVES

Following are the goals for this chapter. Read them, and consider your personal goals. At the end of this chapter, on page 185, you'll list your results.

OBJECTIVES

Business
1. To learn about basic economic indicators
2. To understand how global economic changes can affect your daily life
3. To learn about historical world trade events, and research a current trade agreement.
4. To analyze a changing economy and understand how it impacts international business

Language
5. To understand and be able to use words and expressions related to the global economy
6. To practice your English by discussing an economic issue outside of class
7. To practice using reported speech structures

Personal

_____

_____

_____

Integration

A. GLOBAL ECONOMICS: HEAD-TO-HEAD COMPETITION

The following passage is excerpted from the book, *Head to Head,* 1992, by Lester Thurow, a dean at the Massachusetts Institute of Technology (MIT), professor of economics, and author of several books on world economics. This selection will give you some basic knowledge about how world trade practices impact the global economy. Before you read it, discuss the following questions with an associate. Write your answers on a sheet of paper.

- Why are imported goods usually more expensive than domestically produced goods?
- Name three products that you associate with a particular country. Name the country also.

Threads

Periods during which GDP per head doubled:
Britain, 1780–1838;
U.S., 1839–86;
Japan, 1885–1919;
Korea, 1966–77.

Economist, 10/16/93

A new economic game

by Lester Thurow

Looking backward, future historians will see the twentieth century as a century of niche competition and the twenty-first century as a century of head-to-head competition. . . .

The late 1920s and early 1930s began with a series of worldwide financial crashes that ultimately led to the Great Depression. To preserve jobs, the dominant countries greatly reduced their imports. If only one country had kept imports out, limiting imports would have helped avoid the Great Depression, but with everyone restricting trade, the downward pressures were simply magnified. Fewer imports eventually led to fewer exports. Eventually, those economic blocks evolved into military blocks, and World War II began.

After World War II, the General Agreement on Tariffs and Trade (GATT), was established to prevent a repetition of these events. Trade restrictions and tariff barriers were gradually reduced in a series of trading rounds. Under the rules, each country had to treat all other countries in exactly the same way—the 'most-favored-nation' principle. The best deal—the lowest tariffs, the easiest access, the fewest restrictions—given to one country, must be given to every country.

Balancing America's trading accounts was not a problem. America could grow farm products that the rest of the world could not grow, supply raw materials such as oil that the rest of the world did not have, and manufacture unique high-tech products such as the Boeing 707 that the rest of the world could not build. America's exports did not compete with products

from the rest of the world. They filled gaps that the rest of the world could not fill. In the jargon of today's strategic planners, each country had a noncompetitive niche where it could be a winner. America grew rapidly; the rest of the world grew even more rapidly.

Because of its size, America served as a locomotive for the world economy. Whenever the world sank into a recession, to prevent it from becoming a depression, the United States would stimulate consumer demand—benefiting both American and foreign producers. Foreign exports to America would rise, pulling the exporting countries out of their economic slump. With higher export earnings, these countries would buy more unique American products.

But with success, the American locomotive gradually grew too small to pull the rest of the world. America had gradually shifted from being a large exporter of raw materials, such as oil, to being a large importer. The unique high-tech products that the rest of the world could not build had disappeared in a world of technical equality. They could be gotten many other places. What in the past had been a temporary trade deficit became a permanent trade deficit. Its exports did not automatically rise to balance its imports. A successful noncompetitive niche-export environment had evolved gradually into an intensely competitive head-to-head export environment. . . .

The 1990s start from a very different place. In broad terms there are now three relatively equal contenders—Japan; the European Community, centered around its most powerful country, Germany; and the United States. Starting at approximately the same level of economic development, each country now wants exactly the same industries to ensure that its citizens have the highest standards of living in the twenty-first century. Head-to-head competition is win-lose. Some will win; some will lose. . . .

The competition revolves around the following questions: Who can make the best products? Who expands their standards of living most rapidly? Who has the best-educated and best-skilled workforce in the world? Who is the world's leader in investment—plant and equipment, research and development (R&D), infrastructure? Who organizes best? Whose institutions—government, education, business—are world leaders in efficiency?. . .

Together, America, Japan, and Germany are large enough to be the locomotive pulling the rest of the world into prosperity. If they act together, the rest of the world has little choice but to adopt similar policies. The problem is to get them to work together, when what is good for the world economy is not narrowly good for their own home economies.

Excerpted from Head to Head, by Lester Thurow. William Morrow and Company, Inc., New York, 1992. pp. 29, 55-58.

B. ANALYZING WHAT YOU'VE READ

With a business team, discuss the following questions about the passage you just read. Write the answers on a sheet of paper, using information from the passage and your own ideas.

1. In the 1920s and 1930s, what did the dominant countries do to preserve jobs?
2. Why did "fewer imports eventually lead to fewer exports?"
3. Imagine that your country suddenly kept out imported products. List the products you use that you wouldn't be able to get.
4. Imagine that all other countries suddenly stopped importing products from your country. Which industries in your country would suffer from such trade restrictions?
5. Why was the General Agreement on Tariffs and Trade established?
6. After World War II, the United States could "stimulate consumer demand." How did that policy help other economies? How did it help the U.S. economy?
7. One way a government stimulates consumer demand is to lower interest rates. List some products and/or services you have paid interest on.
8. What type of products did the United States export that the rest of the world needed?
9. Read Paragraph 5 of the reading again. Explain in your own words what a "noncompetitive niche-export environment" is.
10. Thurow says that the niche-export environment was gradually replaced by "head-to-head" competition because the world has become "a world of technical equality." List the technical products you can think of that are now made around the world.

C. JARGON, BUZZWORDS, AND SLANG: WORLD TRADE

Work with an associate. Read the following sentences and discuss the meanings of the underlined noun phrases from the passage. Check your understanding of the underlined phrases by writing a paraphrase for each sentence on a sheet of paper.

LEARNING STRATEGY

Overcoming Limitations: Paraphrasing tests your understanding and extends your vocabulary.

EXAMPLE When the world economy began to slump, the United States would <u>stimulate consumer demand</u> for imports.

Paraphrase: When the world economy slumped, the United States would <u>encourage people to buy</u> imports.

1. In today's global economy, <u>head-to-head competition</u> exists where different countries are competing to control the same industries.
2. As more and more of the world's nations began to produce high-tech products, their need for America's high-tech exports declined. This resulted in a permanent <u>trade deficit</u> for the United States.
3. In a <u>noncompetitive niche-export environment</u>, countries import products that don't compete with their own big industries.
4. When imported products are less expensive than the same products produced domestically, governments will typically raise <u>tariffs</u> on the imported products.
5. In a world of <u>technical equality</u>, many countries are competing to produce the same products at the lowest prices.

D. PUTTING IT ALL TOGETHER

With a business team, review the last three paragraphs of the passage, "A New Economic Game," and complete the following activity.

1. As a team, choose to research Germany, Japan, or the United States. Divide the following topics among team members:
   • Workforce—how well trained and educated?
   • Industries— how productive and technically advanced?
   • Research & development—what areas receive the most government investment?
   • Education—types of programs? percentage of population that is college educated?
   • Infrastructure—how modern are highways and transportation systems?
2. Research your topic. To gather the necessary information, use the sources given in Part I, Exercise D, Item 8. You can also scan the table of contents in various business periodicals for relevant information.

3. With your business team, compile your information to complete the following table for the country you chose. Discuss and take notes in the middle column on the information you find out for each topic. Then, indicate in the right-hand columns whether you feel the country's development in each area is good (+), satisfactory (√), or poor (–).

Country: _____

TOPIC	INFORMATION	+	√	–
Workforce: how well trained and educated?				
Industries: how productive and technically advanced?				
R&D: what areas receive the most government investment?				
Education: types of programs? percent of population college educated?				
Infrastructure: how modern are highways/transportation systems?				

4. Meet with one or two other business team(s) that researched a different country. Discuss the impact of each topic on a country's development. Then come to a consensus on which country has the best rating in each area.

Take a moment to observe a business team coming to a consensus. Check whether you think the participants' level of formality, tone of voice, and nonverbal behavior are appropriate or inapproprate. Also write brief comments or suggestions.

FEATURE	APPROPRIATE	INAPPROPRIATE	COMMENTS AND SUGGESTIONS
Level of Formality			
Tone			
Nonverbal behavior			

E. A CLOSER LOOK AT A CHANGING ECONOMY

Economies are always changing. From a businessperson's view, economic changes can be very important. Learning about economic changes helps businesspeople make decisions about their company's future and their own. In the following passage you will read about Malaysia's changing economy and analyze the effect of these changes on businesses around the world. Before you read, look at the economic indicator graphs for Malaysia on page 179 and discuss the questions that follow with an associate. Write your answers on a sheet of paper.

• Does Malaysia have a trade deficit or a trade surplus? What types of products do you think Malaysia exports? Imports?
• Do you think Malaysia's standard of living has increased or decreased? What information in the graphs helped you decide?
• Traditionally, one of Malaysia's biggest exports has been rubber. List products used around the world in which rubber is a key ingredient.

The Malaysian economy

by Daniel Gaines

Following years of rapid industrialization, Malaysia is now in a period of consolidation. It must manage its success while dealing with a labor shortage, infrastructure bottlenecks, and the threat of inflation. A practical and efficient government hopes to slow growth while diversifying the economy. The country's strengths include minimal corruption and an educated work force. Following is a summary of Malaysia's current economic condition.

EXPORTS
Manufactured

Malaysia is the world's largest exporter of computer chips and the third-largest chip producer, after the United States and Japan. It is home to Intel Corporation's largest overseas plant. The nation has also become a major producer of VCRs and air-conditioning units. By 1991, electrical machinery, appliances and parts had grown to 58% of total exports, which exceeded $40 billion last year.

Natural Resources

Rubber, the principal export, has declined in importance. The land planted with rubber trees has been cut due to falling prices and a labor shortage. In 1991, Indonesia and Thailand surpassed Malaysia as the world's largest rubber producers.

Tin, another traditional export, has declined, making Malaysia the world's fifth—instead of second—largest producer. Of 847 tin mines operating in 1980, only 63 were open in early 1993.

Oil production, on the other hand, has grown significantly. About a quarter of the oil goes to Singapore, while most of the rest is sent to Japan, South Korea, and Thailand. Reserves, especially offshore, are expected to keep production at current levels for at least another decade.

Agriculture

The government has encouraged palm oil production since 1960, and Malaysia is now the largest producer and exporter of the oil, accounting for about 55% of world production in 1992.

EMPLOYMENT

Malaysia is essentially at full employment. There are labor shortages in many areas of industry. The average daily wage was about $6.50 last year, compared to $1.50 in Indonesia and Vietnam. However, Malaysia's skilled workforce is becoming more like those of countries with higher wages, such as Singapore, South Korea, and Taiwan.

CONSUMER DEMAND

Economic growth has created a large lower-middle class that is trying to establish credit to buy durable goods and property. The government, however, is discouraging demand for imported goods by restricting credit. Still, consumer spending is on the rise. Passenger car sales rose a remarkable 32.7% in the third quarter of 1993. A new domestic vehicle factory is beginning operations.

Excerpted and adapted from "The Malaysian Economy."
Los Angeles Times,
March 23, 1994.

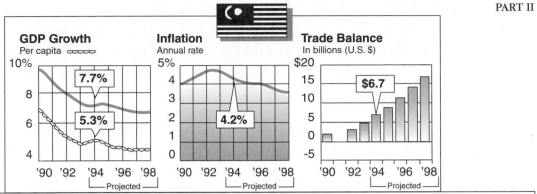

Sources: Bank of America Country Data forecasts: Europa Publications; Economist Intelligence Unit/Bloomberg Financial Markets

Researched by DANIEL GAINES, map by VICTOR KOTOWITZ/Los Angeles Times

LORENA INIGUEZ / Los Angeles Times

F. ANALYZING WHAT YOU'VE READ

With a business team, use the information from the passage to complete the following "Economic Status Report" on Malaysia.

ECONOMIC STATUS REPORT

Country: _Malaysia_

Exports

Manufactured: _Computer chips_

Natural Resources: _____

Agricultural: _____

Growing industries: _____

Declining industries: _____

Account-balance surplus or deficit? _____

Changes in export industries? _____

Employment

Labor: surplus or shortage? _____

Wages: increasing or decreasing? _____

Workforce: educated/skilled? _____

Changes in employment/workforce? _____

Consumer Demand

Type of goods in demand? _____

Demand for imports increasing or decreasing? _____

Government policy on consumer spending? _____

Changes in domestic industry to meet consumer demand? _____

Threads

Malaysian Prime Minister, Dr. Mahathir, plans to raise the number of Malaysian students at university to 30 percent, from 1992's 7 percent, by the end of the decade

Economist, 1/15/94

IT WORKS!
Learning Strategy:
Applying Abstract
Information to
Specific Examples

Using the facts from the Economic Status Report, form logical conclusions to answer the following questions. Write your answers on a sheet of paper.

a. Think about Malaysia's declining export industries. List some products you think are made around the world using these exports.

b. Why do you think these export industries are declining in Malaysia?

c. Consider Malaysia's largest agricultural export. What type of products do you think are made around the world using this export? Which countries might be the largest importers of this export?

d. Consider the employment situation in Malaysia. Do you think the number of foreign companies operating in Malaysia will increase or decrease? Explain.

e. Why do you think the Malaysian government wants to control consumer spending?

G. JARGON, BUZZWORDS, AND SLANG: DESCRIBING ECONOMIC CHANGES

IT WORKS!
Learning Strategy:
Analyzing the
Part You Know
in an Unfamiliar
Two-Word
Expression

Read the following economic expressions from the passage. You are given part of the meaning of each expression. Use the partial meaning to guess at the meaning of the larger, economic expression. Write the completed sentences on a sheet of paper.

period of consolidation	economic diversification
rapid industrialization	infrastructure bottlenecks
labor shortage	

EXAMPLE To "consolidate" is to combine things into a stronger whole, so a "period of consolidation" probably means <u>combining parts of an economy to make it stronger</u>.

1. To "industrialize" is to develop industries, so "rapid industrialization" probably means . . .

2. A "shortage" is not enough of something, so a "labor shortage" probably means . . .

3. To "diversify" is to invest, or be involved in several different enterprises or products, so "economic diversification" probably means . . .

4. A "bottleneck" is a point where traffic or production slows down, so an "infrastructure bottleneck" probably means . . .

Threads

In 1992, nearly $12 billion in foreign investment flowed into China, more than in the three previous years combined.

Worth magazine, April 1994

Now, on a sheet of paper, write a sentence using each of the expressions you just learned. Note that you may have to change the form of the expression to fit the context of your sentence.

EXAMPLE Period of consolidation: *Malaysia is in a period of consolidating many of its industries to become stronger economically.*

1. Rapid industrialization
2. Labor shortage
3. Economic diversification
4. Infrastructure bottleneck

H. PUTTING IT ALL TOGETHER

Economic changes usually affect a country's businesses and its people. In a global economy, economic changes in one country often impact businesses and individuals in other parts of the world too. Imagine that you are the individual described in each of the following situations, and decide what you will do. Choose one of the options given, or decide on your own option.

1. You used to make a living by selling the rubber trees you grew on your land in Malaysia. But in recent years, the price of rubber has been dropping, and the cost of employing workers has increased. You will
   a. sell your land.
   b. use the land for a different enterprise.
   c. live on savings while you wait for the economy to change.

   d. other option: _____

2. You work for a large electronics corporation that has sent you to manage a factory in Malaysia. You do not speak your employees' native language, and they don't speak yours, so you communicate in English. Still, there are cross-cultural communication problems, and you think these problems may be causing your factory's production to drop. You will
   a. hire a cross-cultural consultant.
   b. request more workers from your own country.
   c. give the workers a raise.

   d. other option: _____

3. You are a salesperson for an electronics firm. Your company is deciding whether or not to purchase a large quantity of VCRs from Malaysia at a good price. You feel the products are of high quality but are worried that your customers won't buy them because they are not familiar with Malaysian VCRs. You will
   a. buy them, and tell your customers that the parts are manufactured somewhere else and then assembled in Malaysia.
   b. buy them and put them on sale until Malaysian VCRs become more popular.
   c. wait, and pay a higher price for them later when Malaysian VCRs become more popular.

   d. other option: _____

4. You are an executive for a car manufacturer that exports cars to Malaysia. Sales in Malaysia have been very good. Recently, however, sales have dropped significantly because the Malaysian government has restricted consumer credit. You will

   a. advise the company to stop exporting cars to Malaysia.
   b. advise the company to continue to export cars at lower prices, and wait for the government to stimulate consumer demand for imports.
   c. advise the company to build a new factory in Malaysia in partnership with a Malaysian car company.

   d. other option: _____

Now, discuss and compare your decisions with your associates' decisions in a business team meeting.

I. LISTENING: THE FRIENDSHIP BRIDGE

You are going to listen to a report about growing economic relations between Laos and Thailand. Before you listen, look at Laos and Thailand on the map in Exercise E. Then discuss the following questions with an associate and write your answers on a sheet of paper.

1. Between Laos and Thailand, which country do you think has the largest population? Why?
2. Between Laos and Thailand, which country do you think has the most natural resources? Why?
3. Between Laos and Thailand, which country do you think is more industrialized? Why?

Now, read the following statements. Then listen to the report and decide whether they are true or false.

		T	F
a.	Thailand has 57 million people.	_____	_____
b.	Thailand financed the bridge.	_____	_____
c.	Laos has more forests than Thailand.	_____	_____
d.	Laotian currency is used both in Laos and Thailand.	_____	_____
e.	Laos has decreased its log exports.	_____	_____
f.	Laos has a labor shortage.	_____	_____

[Now, listen to Part I of the report.]

Now, before you listen again, read the following questions. Then listen for the information you need to answer them. Write your answers on a sheet of paper.

1. What natural resources does Thailand get from Laos?
2. What products does Laos get from Thailand?
3. What other countries will probably become economically involved when Laos "opens itself up to the world"?
4. What changes will probably take place in Laos as a result of these new economic relations?
5. What is the attitude of the Laotian government toward its new economic relations with Thailand?

[Repeat Part I of report.]

You will now hear four Laotians comment on the Mitraphap Bridge project. Listen, and take brief notes in the right-hand column on what each person said. The first section is partially completed for you.

SPEAKER	COMMENTS
Government official	*Can't move too slowly*
Hotel owner	
Woman	
Teenager	

[Listen to Part II of report.]

Compare your notes in a business team meeting. Then discuss the following questions and choose the answer, or answers, that you think are most appropriate. For each question think of an additional answer (Choice d) and explain why you think it would also be appropriate.

1. What general attitude about Laos' new economic relations do these comments represent?
   a. Anger
   b. Fear
   c. Enthusiasm

   d. Other: _____

2. How might Laos gain from these economic changes?
   a. More jobs
   b. More natural resources
   c. Higher standard of living

   d. Other: _____

3. How might they lose ?
   a. Fewer jobs
   b. Fewer natural resources
   c. More pollution

   d. Other: _____

J. PUTTING IT ALL TOGETHER

With an associate, research a current international trade agreement or issue. To find necessary information use the following sources:

• World or international business sections of newspapers
• International business, economy, or trade sections of business periodicals

1. Write a brief description of the agreement/issue. What countries are involved? How will the countries be changed?

Communication Memo • Communication Memo • Communication Memo

To: All Employees
From: Corporate Communications Department
Re: Reported Speech

You are going to report on what some people think about an international trade issue. To prepare, review the corporate recommendation on reported speech.

Reported speech, or indirect speech, is written differently from direct speech in the following ways:

- No quotation marks.
- No comma after "said."
- The pronoun changes.
- The word "that" usually introduces the clause that contains what the person said (although "that" can be omitted, especially in informal speech).
- If the actual statement is in the present tense, then the reported speech structure is usually in the past tense.

Direct Speech
A Laotian government official said, "We can't afford to develop as fast as Thailand has."

Reported Speech
A Laotian government official said (that) they couldn't afford to develop as fast as Thailand has.

Enc.
CM/ja

Memo Attachment

Change the following sentences from direct speech to reported speech, writing your sentences on a sheet of paper.

EXAMPLE   Direct speech: He said, "I'm not sure we can afford to take care of all the new roads we're building."

Reported speech: He said that he wasn't sure they could take care of all the new roads they're building.

a. A Laotian government official said, "We can't afford to move too slowly."
b. He also said, "I'm not sure we can take care of all the new roads we are building."
c. A hotel owner said, "I think the bridge is good for business."
d. But he added, "I don't think I'll like the new Laos."
e. A Laotian woman said, "We have a culture where relatives and neighbors provide support for one another."
f. She said, "I don't think you see that in Bangkok."

2. Outside of class, find three native English speakers who are familiar with the international agreement/issue that you researched. Ask them to comment on it, and take notes on what they say.

Share your interview information in a business meeting. Discuss the long-term effects of the trade agreements/issues you researched. How will they affect international businesses? How might they affect you?

PART III

Evaluation

How well did you achieve the objectives for this chapter? List your results on a sheet of paper. Use the prompts that accompany each objective.

OBJECTIVES	RESULTS
Business 1. To learn about basic economic indicators 2. To understand how global economic changes can affect your daily life 3. To learn about historical world trade events, and research a current trade agreement 4. To analyze a changing economy and understand how it impacts international business **Language** 5. To understand and be able to use words and expressions related to the global economy 6. To practice your English by discussing an economic issue outside of class 7. To practice using reported speech structures **Personal** _____ _____ _____	**Business** 1. List the four basic economic indicators you learned about in Part I. 2. Briefly explain how your knowledge of economic growth or decline might affect your career goals (e.g., unemployment, changes in a certain industry). 3. Briefly describe a recent trade issue or agreement and explain its effects on the participating economies. 4. Choose an area researched in Part II, Exercise D, Item 3, and tell which country your group thought had the best "rating"? **Language** 5. Write three sentences that contain the following expressions: trade deficit, rapid industrialization, and economic diversification. 6. Did you enjoy conducting the interview at the end of this chapter? Why or why not? 7. Write two statements based on your out-of-class interview using reported speech structures. **Personal** _____ _____ _____

Now answer the following questions:

• What are your strengths in the area of global economics?
• How can you continue to learn about global economics on your own?